Find the Information You Need!

Find the Information You Need!

Resources and Techniques for Making Decisions, Solving Problems, and Answering Questions

Cheryl Knott

ROWMAN & LITTLEFIELD

Lanham • Boulder • New York • London

Published by Rowman & Littlefield
A wholly owned subsidary of The Rowman & Littlefield Publishing Group, Inc.
4501 Forbes Boulevard, Suite 200, Lanham, Maryland 20706
www.rowman.com

Unit A, Whitacre Mews, 26-34 Stannary Street, London SE11 4AB

British Library Cataloguing in Publication Information Available

Library of Congress Cataloging-in-Publication Data

Names: Knott, Cheryl, 1954- author.
Title: Find the information you need! : resources and techniques for making
    decisions, solving problems, and answering questions / Cheryl Knott.
Description: Lanham : Rowman & Littlefield, [2016] | Includes index.
Identifiers: LCCN 2015039254| ISBN 9781442262478 (hardcover : alk. paper) |
    ISBN 9781442262485 (pbk. : alk. paper) | ISBN 9781442262492 (ebook)
Subjects: LCSH: Electronic information resource searching. | Internet searching. |
    Information resources—Evaluation.
Classification: LCC ZA4060 .K586 2016 | DDC 025.04—dc23
    LC record available at http://lccn.loc.gov/2015039254

∞™ The paper used in this publication meets the minimum requirements of
American National Standard for Information Sciences—Permanence of Paper for
Printed Library Materials, ANSI/NISO Z39.48-1992.

Printed in the United States of America

Contents

PART I: Make It Work

PART II: How and Why It Works

Figures

Tables

Acknowledgments

After teaching a graduate online searching course for years, I began teaching one for undergraduates. Unlike for the graduate course, which had a few great textbooks to choose from, the undergraduate market lacked a user-friendly guide that featured hands-on exercises, clear instruction, and sophisticated but easy-to-learn techniques. Then one day, Rowman & Littlefield executive editor Charles Harmon asked me if I might have an idea for a book. That idea became this book, and I am grateful to Charles for prompting me to go ahead and create the guide I had assumed (and hoped) someone else was in the process of writing. Charles offered good advice and encouragement and helped me persist to the end. I also appreciate the help of assistant editor Robert Hayunga as did production editor Andrew Yoder. Both Charles and Robert kindly and patiently answered my many questions about manuscript preparation.

One of the greatest joys for me on this project has been the opportunity to work with the three-member editorial board for the book: C. Sean Burns, PhD, assistant professor, School of Information Science, College of Communication and Information, University of Kentucky; Ericka J. Patillo, lecturer, School of Information and Library Science, University of North Carolina at Chapel Hill; and Julie Ann Winkelstein, MLIS, PhD, a writer, teacher, and library advocate. Sean, Ericka, and Julie provided comments, suggestions, corrections, and edits that strengthened the book immeasurably. If this text is intelligible and useful, much of the credit goes to them. And if there are errors, they are mine, all mine.

Key points in the text are illustrated with screenshots from various commercial databases, and I am grateful to have received permission to use images from Gale, a part of Cengage Learning, Inc.; EBSCO Industries, Inc.; and Newsbank, Inc. The screenshots and their contents from ABI/Inform Complete and Statistical Insight are published with permission of ProQuest

LLC. Further reproduction is prohibited without permission. Inquiries may be made to ProQuest LLC, 789 E. Eisenhower Pkwy, Ann Arbor, MI 48106-1346. Telephone (734) 761-4700; e-mail, info@proquest.com; web page, www.proquest.com. My thanks go to these corporations and to the other entities, named in the captions, that allowed me to include images from their websites.

Finally, I wish to thank the countless graduate and undergraduate students who have taken my various online searching courses. Their questions, their inquisitiveness, and their dedication to finding the information they need have taught me a great deal about information discovery, and about life in general.

Introduction:
Don't Google That, Do This

Find the Information You Need! is designed for the person who suspects that Google and Facebook and the random clerk at the bookstore aren't always giving them the best information for their specific needs. Created for anyone who wants to understand how to select better information resources, deploy smarter search strategies, and use results more effectively, *Find the Information You Need!* provides

- search exercises on a variety of topics to try yourself;
- coverage of the different types of information resources available, including commercial databases, digital libraries, and open-access repositories;
- clear explanations of search techniques and when and how to use them; and
- helpful advice about evaluating and organizing search results.

This guide to the fundamentals of information discovery can be used as a textbook in undergraduate and graduate online searching courses and as a manual for anyone who wants to move beyond keyword searching on the web. No existing book offers what *Find the Information You Need!* does: a plain-language text that teaches the layperson what information brokers, competitive intelligence professionals, and librarians know about finding authoritative information.

Whether you need to make a decision, solve a problem, answer a question, or write a research report, *Find the Information You Need!* can help by introducing you to the resources, techniques, and practices that professional information searchers use every day. *Find the Information You Need!* will teach you what and how to find the publications and facts that will help you

- decide where to locate your business;
- choose which charities deserve your donations;
- understand what researchers think about issues such as the connection between video games and violent behavior;
- learn whether physical activity might help you get off prescription medications;
- discover what music eighteenth-century Americans liked to dance to, and where to find that music now; and
- bunches of other topics.

Find the Information You Need! can be used by high school and under-graduate students undertaking research assignments. It treats your assignment as a quest for information that anyone in the real world of business, government, the sciences, journalism, and other fields might undertake. Consequently, anyone with a serious need for information can benefit from using the techniques described in this book. *Find the Information You Need!* can even help you win bets at your local bar: world's tallest building, oldest person, ugliest dog? The answer from the most up-to-date, authoritative source wins!

If you've come this far, chances are you have mastered Google search but have a nagging feeling you might be missing something. You may be missing huge amounts of information, for two reasons. First, most current publications are copyrighted and not freely available, so search engines can't retrieve them from behind paywalls unless you or an institution you're affiliated with pays. Second, search engines are designed to learn your interests and preferences and favor those in your results. You end up in what Internet activist Eli Pariser calls a "filter bubble" that tends not to introduce you to new ideas or sources.[1] In addition to missing out on information that might be useful, you may be giving away more data than you're getting back, since most search engines track your clicks and share your queries and movements with other companies and the federal government.

Sure, searching the web is convenient and easy. Lots of times it's all you need to find the recipe, the high-school sweetheart, or the movie synopsis you're seeking. For important projects, however, there are better ways to find the authoritative, reliable, detailed information you need.

Because we're all used to the immediate gratification of web searching, this book is designed so that you can dip into it at any point and learn something quickly. No need to work your way in a linear fashion from beginning to end. You can browse the pages or use the table of contents at the front and the keyword index at the back to help you locate a particular topic or method. Working through the book from beginning to end has its advantages, though, because you'll begin with actual search experiences and then look under the hood to see why those searches worked the way they did. *Find the Information You Need!* is organized into two main sections. Part I, "Make It Work," helps you become a better searcher right away by giving you practical exercises to try. The six chapters in part I focus on concrete steps to take for results and gives only as much explanation as needed to prevent confusion. The six chapters in part II, "How and Why It Works," provide technical details and explanations of search systems and retrieval methods. Feel free to start with chapter 1 and then skip to chapter 8 or chapter 9 if you want to know more about why one of the exercises in chapter 1 worked the way it did. Or, if you want background first, read all the chapters in part II, then try the activities in part I. Or you may want to cruise through the first seven chapters, picking up search tips and techniques you can use over and over again, and never get around to reading the technical details in the second half of the book.

However you approach this text, do take a look at the three appendixes at the end. That's where you will discover the most valuable resources and be able to use your newly acquired search skills to find the information you need. Appendix I focuses on commercial databases accessible at no charge to you via your state library agency. Most taxpayers don't know their state government includes a library agency, so discovering that you can visit the state library's website and find freely available databases containing authoritative information makes this appendix a great reference. Appendix II lists freely available encyclopedias, including not only *Wikipedia* but many others that are more focused and more authoritative. Appendix III provides links to a variety of information resources, including health-related data and guidance from U.S. government agencies, huge digital libraries from major educational institutions, and other troves of knowledge treasures.

SOME BASIC TERMS AND DEFINITIONS

Since chapter 1 jumps right into a search exercise, it's useful here to give a few definitions. These are explained in more detail in part II, but the basics are here for you to skim now and return to later if needed.

A *database* is a collection of records. In this book, most of the databases discussed are bibliographic databases, with "bibliographic" meaning anything related to texts such as books, book chapters, book reviews, articles, stories, doctoral dissertations, master's theses, transcripts of broadcasts or spoken testimony, and reports. A few databases are not "bibliographic" but instead are numeric (e.g., giving statistics related to the U.S. economy) or audiovisual (e.g., including digital photographs or sound recordings). I also refer to commercial or proprietary databases, which are produced by for-profit companies that charge fees for using them.

A *database record* is a record that represents a book or article (or other information object) by providing basic data about it: author, title, publisher, date, and so forth. Each record follows a consistent template for arranging the information; the author name is always input in the box for author names, the title is always input in the title box, and so forth. Most records include an abstract that summarizes the contents of the information object. The record might include a few subject headings or subject descriptors, terms that the human beings creating the records added to make it more likely you'll find them. In some databases, the record includes the full text of the article. The main thing to know about "full text" is that, if a database offers access to full text, that means you don't have to go anywhere else, such as to a physical library or a magazine's pay-to-view website, to read the whole article.

An *index* is a tool for making concepts, topics, and other kinds of information findable. You're probably familiar with checking the back of a book for an index that lists keywords in alphabetical order along with the page numbers on which they appear. A bibliographic database as a whole is an index, in the sense that it makes it possible for you to find, as one example, an article in a magazine, no matter what issue it was published in. All of the meaningful keywords on a database record are indexed so you can find every record (every information object) that uses the keywords you are interested in.

A *search system* is a combination of automated components that makes it possible for you to query a database and retrieve the records relevant to your query terms. The search system includes interfaces such as the screen you see when you search and the screen you see when results are presented to you. The search system includes the search engine, an automated program that matches the terms you input in the search box to the records in the database and shows you only the records that match your terms. You can think of the search system as the mediator between you and the information you seek; getting to know the mediator will help you find what you seek.

A *search query* consists of the search terms you input and the techniques you use to combine your terms and filter the results. It represents a translation of your topics and questions into a form the search engine can apply to the database you have chosen to use.

A FEW MORE TIPS

Throughout the book, search terms are shown in *italics*. In many systems, putting quotation marks around two or more keywords tells the system to search the phrase rather than the individual words; phrase searches will include these quotation marks in *italics*. The features and link labels shown on the screens, such as the question mark icon for help and the button next to a search box labeled with a command such as "search" or "submit," are shown in **bold**.

Two pieces of advice about the search examples that follow. First, I'm concentrating on a few of the biggest and most common databases. You'll learn a lot about those databases and how to use them. But you can generalize your learning to other databases. The examples are designed to teach the specifics about a particular database and the kinds of features and techniques you can use with any database search system, even ones you've never seen before. Once you learn what to expect when you search, you'll know what to look for, even if a database is new to you. Second, databases are redesigned once in a while, so it's possible the actual database screen you see when you try a search will look different from the screenshots included with my search examples. I'll announce those kinds of changes and updates on twitter.com, so you may want to follow me, @findinfouneed, or occasionally skim my stream of tweets. Stay flexible and inquisitive, and be willing to experiment and analyze the results. And don't be like some infamous drivers who never stop to ask for directions. Know that every database has a built-in help system and use it when, or even before, you get lost.

NOTES

1. Eli Pariser, *The Filter Bubble: What the Internet Is Hiding from You* (New York: Penguin Press, 2011).

PART I

Make It Work

CHAPTER 1

Magazines and Newspapers in General-Interest Databases

Obviously, you can use a web search engine like Google to find good information mixed in with the advertising and the sites trying to sell you products. But wouldn't it be nice to have some solid magazine and newspaper articles with information that you know is from reliable sources and edited by able experts? And wouldn't it be lovely to find them from your own home without having to go to the library, the bookstore, or the newsstand? Yes. And yes.

Luckily for us, there's a whole industry devoted to indexing magazines, newspapers, broadcast news programs, and other information items including books. In this chapter, we'll use one of the biggest and most popular indexes to a wide variety of information sources from all over the world, General OneFile. An index makes it possible to discover an article that appeared in an issue of a magazine, a story published in a newspaper, or an item discussed on a television or radio news program. Computerized indexes (or databases, as they are called in this book) make each meaningful word (not common little words like *the* and *it* and *of*) searchable. So you can search a word and trust the index (the database) to find it, then show you the articles or stories that word appears in. Depending on the database, it might show you the citation to the item and let you track down the actual item in your local library, or it might give you access to the full text or video by simply clicking on a link.

Chapter X {**AU: ?**} explains more about indexing, but for now the main point is to understand that a database like General OneFile indexes a particular selection of popular magazines, academic journals, books, and broadcasts—in this case it's a big selection of more than 13,000 periodicals and other sources—making it possible for you to find information about the topics you are researching.

By the time you finish the activities in this chapter, you will

- know how to use quotation marks to search for phrases;
- understand how to evaluate a set of results and use filters for better results;
- be able to access full text of articles within databases; and
- have experience searching two widely available, general-interest databases that index a lot of major magazines and newspapers.

Your task as a seeker, and finder, of information is to translate your research topic into a language and a strategy the search system can use effectively. Your goal is to strike a balance between retrieving too many results and not enough. In other words, you want to craft a search that makes the system do all the hard work of winnowing out irrelevant stuff. At the same time, you want to craft a search that brings back all of the relevant stuff and maybe a little irrelevant stuff to reassure you that nothing important is left out. This is a science and an art and a process, and you'll get better at it. But no one ever gets to that place where all his or her searches are perfect the first time. Let's get started with a real search.

SEARCH ACTIVITY: GREEN HOUSING

A lot of cities and towns are experiencing growth in new housing. With climate change and increasing utility costs, it might be wise to create green housing. Whether you are a college student writing a research paper for a course, a government employee looking to formulate policies to encourage green building, or a consumer considering building your own environmentally friendly home, recent magazine and newspaper articles will be of use.

You might know of a few magazines likely to have features about green housing, such as *Mother Earth News* and *Better Homes and Gardens*. Perhaps your local newspaper has run a story about an environmental builder in your city. You could spend a lot of time trying to find those articles by browsing through the magazines and newspapers you know about. The advantage of using an index is that you can search many magazines and newspapers, including many you've never heard of, all at once.

We'll start with General OneFile, which indexes both *Mother Earth News* and *Better Homes and Gardens*, along with more than 7,000 other periodicals and newspapers, going back about three decades. That might sound a little overwhelming, but we're going to use some techniques to retrieve exactly what we want. These are common techniques, so once you learn them in the General OneFile database, you can use them in others. A quick-and-dirty search for *green homes*—the same kind of search you might try with Google—will retrieve more results than we can use, but it will give us a sense of what has been published and how we can narrow down our search.

To try these techniques as we go along, open a web browser on whatever networked device you are using (desktop or laptop computer, tablet, smartphone). Use appendix I to find the URL for your state library's list of databases available to state residents, then log in to General OneFile. If the database is not accessible that way, try your local public or college library website. You may have to actually go to a physical library to be able to use the database, and if so, don't forget to take this book with you to practice the activities. If General OneFile is not available to you at all, do not be alarmed. We'll cover other databases that you will be able to use, and this section of the book introduces you to a few key concepts you can use with any database.

Look closely at figure 1.1, which shows the basic search screen you'll see when you log in to the General OneFile database. I have added seven numbered boxes to help you get oriented to this search interface:

1. A plain white search box, similar to Google's, where you can type in your terms and then click on the magnifying glass icon to the right to activate the search.
2. A little arrow in the search box leading to a pull-down menu for limiting your search. The default is a **Keyword** search, but clicking the downward arrow opens up other options, such as searching by author instead of keyword.
3. **Subject Guide Search** helps you identify the best terms for your topic.
4. **Publication Search** helps you find a specific magazine and its contents.
5. You can use the **Popular Articles** links to read about items of interest to other users of the database.
6. The **Topic Finder** provides a visual depiction of the most important search terms for your topic. Like the **Subject Guide Search** (no. 3), it might help you find better terms than the first keywords that occur to you.
7. **Trending Now** can link you immediately to articles on timely topics. Like the **Popular Articles** links (no. 5), this feature can help students decide on a topic for an upcoming research paper assignment.

SEARCH STRATEGIES AND RESULTS

Log in to the General OneFile database to follow along on our search for articles about green housing, the idea that people's homes can be environmentally friendly. You can already guess that searching for *green housing*

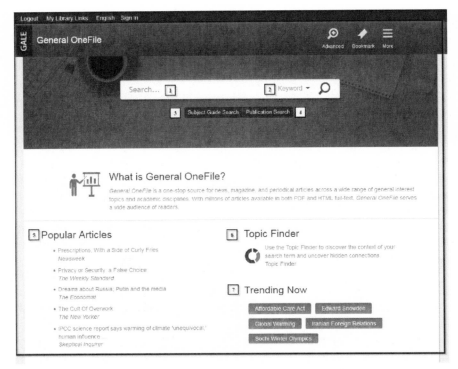

Figure 1.1. Basic search screen. From General OneFile. © Gale, a part of Cengage Learning, Inc. Reproduced by permission www.cengage.com/permissions.

might be a bit tricky, since the word *green* has other meanings besides "environmentally friendly." To see how tricky, go ahead and input *green housing* in the search box and click the magnifying glass icon.

The system will retrieve multiple results—and remember, most of these are articles under copyright and therefore not accessible on the open web. Because the search system retrieves anything that mentions our two words, not all of these results will be about green housing in the way we mean it. We'll have better luck if we tell the system to search those two words next to each other and in that order: in other words, as a phrase. By putting quotation marks around our two words, we force the computer system to search the phrase *"green housing"* rather than the word *green* anywhere and the word *housing* anywhere.

If you've been trained by Google, you might skim the first screen of results, pick a few that look okay, and call it a day. That works with Google because of its relevance ranking system and its tracking of your preferences and interests, so results offered at the top of the list are likely to answer your question. Some databases, such as those on the ProQuest platform, follow

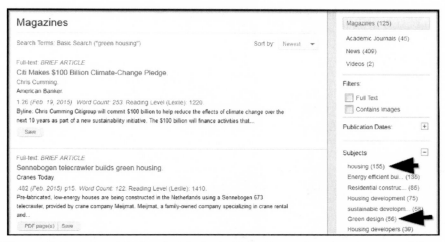

Figure 1.2. Beginning of the list of results for the "Green Housing" search, with a menu of filters on the right. The two arrows in the lower right point to the best official subject descriptors for this topic. From General OneFile. © Gale, a part of Cengage Learning, Inc. Reproduced by permission www.cengage.com/permissions.

Google's lead by presenting results in order of their relevance to your query. General OneFile shows you results in a different order, with the most recently published ones first. Recent is nice, especially for current events, but if an article isn't about your topic, it doesn't matter how new it is. Happily, there are lots of ways to eliminate results you don't want instead of browsing through hundreds of results to find the ones you do want.

One of the most obvious ways to limit results to what we want is to decide what we want. One of the great aspects of an all-purpose index like General OneFile is that it includes all kinds of articles, not only from popular and trade magazines, but also from academic journals, newspapers, videos, and audios. Our *"green housing"* search was broad, but the screen of results includes some filters on the right-hand side that are quite helpful (see figure 1.2).

The first category, "Magazines," tells us that 45 of our results are from academic journals, while 409 are news stories. These are clickable links, so if you only want to see the 45 academic articles, click on the line for that. You can use the checkboxes to see only articles where the entire full text is immediately available from inside the database and to see only the ones that include images. You can click on the little plus signs to see more, as I have done for "Subjects." Two of the subjects seem right on target for this search, *housing* and *green design*. If you click on the *housing* link, you can see the 155 articles about housing. If you click on the *green design* link, you can see the 56 articles about that. But we don't want either or; we want both.

Let's take our newfound knowledge back to the search box. This time, we'll type *green design and housing and united states* and use the downward arrow to the right to switch from Keyword to Subject. I added the geographic subject, United States, because this database indexes foreign magazines and newspapers, and I'm not so interested in green housing in China or India. (You don't have to capitalize names like United States because the search system doesn't know the difference.) As you can see in figure 1.3, the results are actually about green housing in the United States.

The third result looks great. It's a longish article of almost three thousand words about a new home with so many attractive energy-efficient features that it won an award. Results further down on the list discuss earth-sheltered homes and efforts to build energy-efficient homes using solar and other techniques. These are all excellent stories for consumers thinking about building their own green homes. Plus, they give us some new terms to search such as *"earth-sheltered homes"* and *"energy efficient homes"* that we

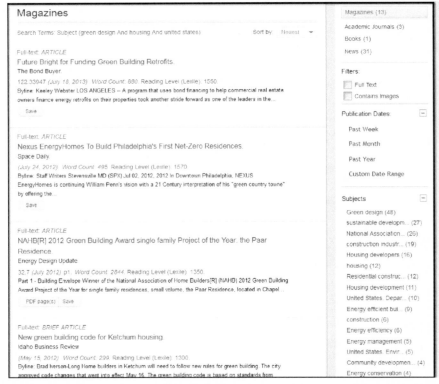

Figure 1.3. Beginning of the list of results for the subject search *green design and housing* and menu of filters on the right. From General OneFile. © Gale, a part of Cengage Learning, Inc. Reproduced by permission www.cengage.com/permissions.

can use to go back to the search box, input as phrases, and switch back to keyword searching (instead of subject searching, which can be limiting when you are trying a new topic).

Instead of searching each different kind of home separately, you can put the word *or* between each phrase to retrieve one set of results with articles about the different kinds. In the basic search box, you can input

"solar homes" or "straw bale homes" or "earth sheltered homes" or "energy efficient homes"

to retrieve articles and stories that mention at least one of those phrases. Again, you can use the filters on the right to limit your results further.

To move past the list of results and actually read some of the articles, simply click on the title of the article to link to the full text. As figure 1.3 shows, all the results whose titles link you to the article itself are labeled **Full-text**.

Figure 1.4 shows a list of three different kinds of results for a search on *solar houses*.

The first result in figure 1.4 is only a citation for an article by Douglas Brown, titled "Boxed Canyon" and published on page 108 of the January–February 2014 issue of *Sierra* magazine, volume 99, issue number 1. The citation gives you all the information you need to be able to find the article, but the article itself is not included in this database. The title of the article is a link; it goes to a short synopsis or abstract of the article. You have a couple of choices for finding the article itself. You can check your local library catalog to see if your library has *Sierra* magazine in its collection. If you do that, look up the magazine title, not the article title. Remember, General OneFile is an index that lets us find articles in magazines. A library catalog tells us whether the library owns the magazines, but not what's in them. If the magazine is listed in the catalog, you can pay a visit to the library, find the magazine volumes on the shelves, pluck issue 1 of volume 99 off the shelf, and open it to page 108 to see Douglas Brown's short article.

The second result in figure 1.4 is labeled **Audio**, and if you click on the icon, you'll be able to listen to a radio broadcast from the PBS program *All Things Considered* about a Florida island where homeowners rely on solar energy because the island is not on the electrical grid. A transcript of the program is included in the link if you want to read it instead of or in addition to hearing it.

The last result in figure 1.4 is for the full text of an article in *Natural Life* magazine. Clicking on the title takes you to the full text, with photographs of cutting-edge solar houses and a button labeled **Listen**, if you want to hear the story read instead of reading it yourself. Rather than clicking on the title from the results list, you can activate the little **PDF** button at the bottom of the citation to save the article to your computer.

Figure 1.4. Three different kinds of results (circled): a citation to an article, an audio file, and the full text of an article. From General OneFile. © Gale, a part of Cengage Learning, Inc. Reproduced by permission www.cengage.com/permissions.

DIFFERENT DATABASE, SAME TECHNIQUES

If your state or local library does not provide access to General OneFile, it probably offers a similar database, such as MasterFILE Premier. Although MasterFILE Premier is not as big as General OneFile, you can find a lot of publications on your topic, because it indexes about seventeen hundred periodicals and includes the full text for most of the articles in them. In addition, MasterFILE Premier indexes about five hundred reference books and includes other kinds of material such as images. We used General OneFile

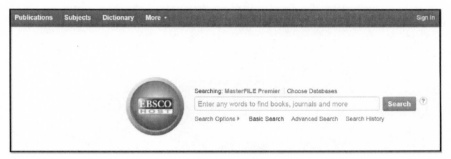

Figure 1.5. MasterFile Premier basic search screen. © 2015 EBSCO Industries, Inc. Used with permission of EBSCO Information Services.

on the Gale Cengage platform. MasterFILE Premier is on the EBSCOhost platform. Gale Cengage and EBSCOhost are competitors in the database industry, and you can see right away in figure 1.5 that their search interfaces are quite different from each other. Even though the two platforms present a different look and feel, their underlying search systems offer many of the same functions and features.

Even though the look and feel of the MasterFILE Premier basic search screen differs from General OneFile's, both offer many of the same search features. So let's begin by using quotation marks around our topic *"green housing"* to force the system to search the phrase rather than separate keywords. Using quotation marks for phrase searching is common to many search engines, including Google.

MasterFILE Premier displays results down the middle of the screen, but its filters are to the left. On offer are the same kinds of filters as you'll find with other databases, such as type of publication and subject terms. Figure 1.6 shows a few of the sixty-nine results for our *"green housing"* search. The first arrow points to the filter showing that forty-one of the results are from magazines. The second arrow points to a subject term we might want to use for this topic, *ecological houses*. Although databases offer many of the same kinds of tools and features, they don't necessarily use the same terminology for subjects. For example, the subject term we discovered in General OneFile, *green design*, is not a subject term in MasterFILE Premier. You can still use *green design* in MasterFILE Premier, but only as a keyword type of search. You would get no results if you tried using *green design* as a subject in MasterFILE Premier.

Remember how General OneFile's search screen provided a downward arrow to the right of the search box where we could change from the default keyword search to a subject search? MasterFILE Premier offers the same feature, just not on its basic search screen. Change to the advanced search

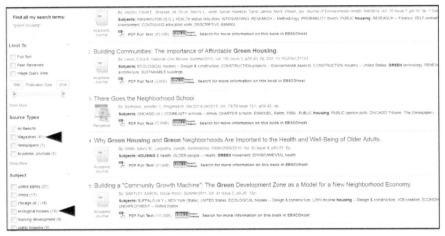

Figure 1.6. Results for *"green housing"* search in MasterFILE Premier with filtering tools on the left. The arrows point to the filter for magazine articles and the filter for the items tagged with the official subject descriptor *ecological houses.* © 2015 EBSCO Industries, Inc. Used with permission of EBSCO Information Services.

screen by clicking on the link labeled, you guessed it, **Advanced Search**, right under the search box, to see more options.

The advanced search screen provides three search boxes. With a complex topic, such as the economic impact of ecological houses in the Pacific Northwest, we could put the different concepts or aspects in the different search boxes. But it's okay to use only one search box, as in figure 1.7. There's the downward arrow over to the right of each search box, and we have used it to search our subject term *"ecological houses"* (which we discovered when we did our *"green housing"* search). Again, the left-side menu offers filters; I have closed all but the **Subject** one so you can see some of the subjects included in our results. For example, 103 of the 524 results are about ecological houses in the United States. If you want to see only those 103, click on that link in the **Subjects** list, and the database will show them to you.

You've probably already figured out that each article title in our results list is a link. Click on it to see the complete citation and the summary or abstract of the article. The full text of the article, including images and illustrations, is available from the results list by clicking on the **PDF Full Text** icon under each result. If there's no PDF icon, the full text is not in the database, and you'll need to check your local library's catalog to see if you can find the magazine there. In figure 1.7, the first and third results have PDF icons that take you to the full text of those articles, but the second one doesn't.

Figure 1.7. Advanced search for *"ecological houses"* as a subject term, with the first few results down the middle of the screen and filtering options on the left. From MasterFile Premier. © 2015 EBSCO Industries, Inc. Used with permission of EBSCO Information Services.

APPRECIATING DIFFERENCES

We searched two different databases on two different platforms. With both, we used

- quotation marks for phrase searching,
- filters to discover subject terms for our topics,
- pull-down menus to change from keyword to subject searching, and
- PDF icons to access complete articles.

The search and results screens looked different, but we were able to take what we learned from our first experience with database searching and apply it to our second experience. Because both databases are large and index thousands of periodicals and some books and other material, we can get useful material from either one of them for almost any research project we have. Between the two, some of our searches might even retrieve identical articles, since these two large databases index some of the same periodicals. But they don't always use the same subject terms for topics, so it's good to use the method we have used in this chapter to discover good articles: start with your best guess regarding the keywords for your topic, then let the results and filters help you find even better ones (or maybe reassure you that your search terms are the best for the topic after all).

Don't stop with these two databases. You may have free access to others via your state or local library, as well as to databases for newspapers only (no magazines, no book chapters). Whatever databases you have access to, after completing the search activities in this chapter, you should be feeling confident in your ability to craft a search that yields results you can use.

WHY IT WORKS

We used large general-interest databases indexing lots of magazine, journal, news, and media sources.

We searched phrases to get better results than we would have with keyword-anywhere searches.

We used filters to identify subject descriptors and pull-down menus to search subject terms rather than keywords.

Good point: It's a great idea to slow down and look carefully at the search and the results screens for hints about ways to home in on exactly the information you need.

CHAPTER 2

Research Riches

A magazine or newspaper is written for a mass or popular audience, in contrast to a scholarly journal, which is written for academics, researchers, and experts. Several features distinguish scholarly journals from other kinds of periodicals: their narrow but deep coverage of a subject, peer reviewing of articles before they are accepted for publication, and the published articles' citations to other published articles on the same topic. In college, students are usually expected to use scholarly literature rather than popular magazines when writing term papers. Scholarly articles are important sources of information used by researchers in business and industry, the health sciences, the arts and humanities, and the social sciences. When people talk about standing on the shoulders of giants, they often mean their research accomplishments have built on the research of others who came before them. Finding earlier research as well as current articles on a topic can help you understand an issue well enough to form knowledgeable opinions about it, to ask your own questions regarding it, and to design and carry out research to address those questions.

By the time you finish the activities in this chapter you will

- know how to distinguish a scholarly journal from a popular periodical,
- understand how to craft a search strategy for scholarly research topics,
- use results to find additional material related to your topic, and
- have experience searching two widely available academic databases that index many scholarly journals.

SCHOLARLY-NESS

How can you recognize a scholarly journal? Consider its name, its editorial board members, and how its articles look. The name is usually a dead giveaway, because most scholarly journals have the word "journal" in their title. Examples are *Journal of Applied Microbiology, Journal of Asian Economics, Texas Hispanic Journal of Law and Policy*, and *Computing & Control Engineering Journal*. A third category of periodicals, trade journals, sometimes have the word "journal" in their titles, too. A trade journal serves a particular industry and often includes news about the major players and events in that industry. Scholarly journals focus on research instead. Some don't have the word journal in their titles, but you can tell they are focused on a fairly narrow academic topic: *Feminist Media Studies, MIS Quarterly, Music Education Research*, and *Chemistry & Biodiversity*.

Another way to identify a scholarly journal is to look at the information about the journal in the front of an issue or on the journal's website. The "about" will include the names, titles, and institutional affiliations of the editorial board members, most of whom are probably professors at colleges and universities or scientists at labs or other research institutions. Yet another way is to look at the articles in a scholarly journal; all of the substantive research articles will include footnotes, endnotes, or bibliographies (or all three) citing the sources the authors used. Magazines and newspaper articles cite their sources, but those sources are usually people the writer interviewed, and their statements are woven into the text of the article. The readers of a popular magazine or newspaper want to know who said what. The readers of a scholarly journal want to know who published what where, so they can read that material too and possibly even cite it in their own publications if it relates to their own research.

You can probably find citations to a lot of this material using the web-based index to scholarly articles, Google Scholar, https://scholar.google.com. A Google Scholar record for an article in a scholarly journal may give you a link to the journal publisher's website, where you can access the citation and the abstract (a short summary of the article) for free, but where a paywall separates you from the full text (or from your money if you choose to pay). Google Scholar might give you a link to a version of the full text of the article that the author has deposited in an open-access repository. Maybe half the citations you find using Google Scholar will include a link to such a freely accessible version of the article.[1]

When a citation doesn't have a link to the full text of the article, you have to go to your library's website and access a database offering not only indexing but also full-text access. Consequently, starting at Google Scholar may actually create extra effort or extra steps in some cases.

Learning which databases are available and which ones index which journals can save time, help you get access to full articles without paying fees, and help you discover material not indexed (yet) by Google Scholar. You'll find the proprietary search engines and the value-added information structure and organization of the commercial databases much more powerful at retrieving relevant and precise results than the sort of quick-and-dirty approach of Google Scholar. Don't get me wrong: I love Google Scholar. I do know, however, when to save myself a lot of work by going straight to a database accessible from the library's website. This may be changing, though, because Google Scholar and ProQuest, yet another database vendor, have teamed up so that material indexed in ProQuest databases will also appear on Google Scholar results screens. If you are a college or university student, Google Scholar may recognize your computer's unique address on the Internet and give you access to full-text articles in ProQuest databases your institution subscribes to, after you sign in with your student ID and password.

Scholarly journals are indexed in databases similar to the two used in chapter 1. We used the Gale Cengage General OneFile, and it has a scholarly sister database, Academic OneFile. We used EBSCO's MasterFILE Premier, and it has a scholarly sister, Academic Search Complete. General OneFile and Academic OneFile do overlap with each other a bit, and MasterFILE Premier and Academic Search Complete overlap with each other a little. As you learned in chapter 1, you can do a search in General OneFile, then use the filters to select only the scholarly articles. Similarly, MasterFILE Premier's advanced search screen offers a little checkbox you can click to retrieve only peer-reviewed articles, leaving out the popular periodicals. If you know you want only scholarly material, though, it's more efficient to use a scholarly database such as Academic OneFile or Academic Search Complete.

Both Academic OneFile and Academic Search Complete index scholarly journals on a variety of subjects/topics. Gale's Academic OneFile indexes more than nine thousand peer-reviewed journals and gives you the full text of many of the indexed articles, and it includes other kinds of material as well, such as transcripts of radio and television broadcasts. EBSCO's Academic Search Complete is a gargantuan database, indexing more than twelve thousand journals and supplying full text of articles from more than eight thousand of them. It includes some monographs (books on focused scholarly subjects), reports, and conference proceedings.

ASPIRE TO SEARCH SYSTEMATICALLY

We're going to use "ASPIRE" as a way to remember the elements of systematic searching. Think of these as six steps that help your quest for information become a reliable search method, no matter the topic or question:

Assume that an answer to your research questions can be found.
Select the best available database for the topic.
Plan your search strategy in advance.

Inspect several results from your initial search to learn how you might
refine your strategy for better results.

Revise your initial research questions, if needed, and your initial search
query as you learn more about your topic from the information you
are retrieving.

Evaluate your results and select the most authoritative and relevant ones
to download and use.

Assuming that an answer or answers can be found helps you persist in
searching for and ultimately finding the information you want. Information
seekers sometimes have a small mental image of the totality of published
knowledge, and if their first try doesn't yield good results, they think they
have exhausted the possibilities and give up. Don't let that happen to you.

Selecting the best database for the job saves time and ensures success.
Knowing there are hundreds of databases to choose from should encourage
you to check your library's website to see if the available indexes are sorted
into subject-oriented categories that you can use as a guide. You can check
the help or about screens to see what kind of information is indexed in a
database, what the time period coverage is, and whether material in languages other than English is included. You can use the "ask a librarian" chat
function on a library's website to get good advice about the best database to
use for your question or research project.

Planning in advance is more efficient than winging it, especially when
you are researching a topic that you are still learning about. Crafting a query
that transforms your research question into a search the database system
can perform involves a few minutes of critical thinking and preparation.
Perhaps you have an internship with an oil and gas company engaged in
fracking, or maybe you are taking an environmental studies course and you
want to write a formal report on the effects of fracking on nearby water
sources. Your research question might be "What are the effects of fracking
on groundwater?" Sure, you'll get results if you input *fracking and groundwater*. But the search will work better if you take a minute to translate your
keywords into terms that retrieve exactly the right articles for your formal
report. Sketch out a table in which the first column contains the different
concepts of the question and the rows contain synonyms for and facets of
the concepts, using table 2.1 as your guide.

Two ways of combining search terms involve two little words known as
Boolean operators. In the search phrase *fracking and groundwater*, the Boolean operator is *and*. It tells the search engine to find all the records that
have the word *fracking*, find all the records that have the word *groundwater*,
then combine those two sets of records and show only the ones that include
both. In table 2.1, the Boolean *and* is used between the different concepts
(or terms) in the first column. The other important Boolean operator is *or*.

Table 2.1. Worksheet showing terms and their synonyms or facets for a research question related to the topic of fracking

Different Facets	Synonym No. 1	Synonym No. 2	Synonym No. 3
fracking	hydraulic fracturing		
groundwater	water	aquifer	river
effects	contamination	pollution	

It is used to make sure our set of records includes synonyms for our topic. In table 2.1, the Boolean *or* is used between the terms in the rows, like this:

fracking or hydraulic fracturing
groundwater or water or aquifer or river
effects or contamination or pollution

The three different sets of results can then be combined with the Boolean operator *and* between them.

Such an approach should give you some good results, and inspecting a few of the most promising ones might yield ideas for homing in on the best information in the database. One important element to look for in the most relevant records is a list of subject descriptors. In our example, you would quickly discover that *hydraulic fracturing* is a subject descriptor and so is *water pollution*. Subject descriptors take the guesswork out of crafting a search query; no need to dream up all the possible synonyms, plurals, or British spellings to make sure you're not missing something. Instead, you can do a subject search by using the pull-down menu next to the search boxes to change from the default keyword to the subject search, then input the correct descriptors. Figure 2.1 shows what that looks like in Academic Search Complete.

Inspecting early results gives you a chance to learn not only which subject descriptors you should use, but also what sorts of questions experts are

Figure 2.1. Advanced search screen showing pull-down menus changed to SU Subject Terms so the system will look only in the subject field of all the records in the database for the descriptors. From MasterFile Premier. © 2015 EBSCO Industries, Inc. Used with permission of EBSCO Information Services.

asking about the topic. And revising your research questions means keeping an open mind as you learn what interests the experts.

You may find that not many results have been published in academic journals; when I applied that filter to the search for the two subject descriptors, there were not enough results for my report. I know water is a huge issue when it comes to fracking, though. Apparently researchers are framing their questions a bit differently than my rather narrow focus on water pollution. When I take the word *pollution* out of my query, I get more results and find some good articles in which the researchers focus on methods for treating and reclaiming water used in the fracking process.

Evaluating your final set of results helps you know which ones to actually use for your purposes. Read the abstracts to get a sense of the scope of the article, notice the publication year to make sure you're getting up-to-date information, and consider whether the author provides a broad overview or a deep dive into the topic.

Because finding the correct subject descriptors for a concept or topic can save you a lot of trouble, let's spend a little more time discussing them.

A THESAURUS OF TERMS

You may be familiar with *Roget's Thesaurus* and/or the thesaurus in your word-processing software. We often use these to make ourselves sound smarter when we are writing a paper by replacing a commonly used word for a synonym that makes it sound like we are masters of a more sophisticated vocabulary. There is another kind of thesaurus, though. It lists all of the preferred terms for different concepts and topics in a particular academic discipline or subject area that an authoritative group of scholars has agreed to use. These preferred terms are called "subject headings" or "subject descriptors" to distinguish them from plain old natural language keywords. You may have used Library of Congress Subject Headings, descriptors for books listed in library catalogs. In a commercial database that indexes articles in periodicals and chapters in books, it's more common to refer to "descriptors" rather than "subject headings."

Sometimes a keyword is the same as the descriptor; water pollution is water pollution. In that case, what makes the difference is limiting the search to the subject field, because that means you'll retrieve only the items for which the descriptor was added to the record because the article is truly about that topic. In other words, there could be an article about air pollution with a title like "Beyond Water Pollution: Why the Air Should Be Our Main Concern Now." It casually mentions water pollution, but it's not actually about water pollution. If you did a broad keyword search for water pollution, you'd retrieve this article along with a lot of others. Then you'd have to sort through them and decide for yourself which are really about water pollution. If you use a subject descriptor and you limit your search to the subject field, you won't retrieve items like that, and you won't have to waste your time sorting through the irrelevant material.

Why do we need such thesauri? Because our natural language—the language we use every day—is messy and confusing. Do you watch movies, videos, films, moving pictures, or motion pictures? If you are researching that kind of stuff in a full-text database with no thesaurus, then here's your only option if you want to be thorough: you would have to input a search string using the Boolean *or* operator to make sure you are retrieving all relevant records, no matter what the author called this concept in the title or abstract. And you'd have to take into consideration that some might refer to the movie industry or the film business, so you'd need to have singular and plural as well. It would look like this:

movie or movies or video or videos or film or films or moving picture or moving pictures or motion picture or motion pictures

That's one big boatload of typing. How much more efficient would it be to have an agreed-on term for this whole raft of labels for what is essentially all the same thing? A lot! You could look up one of these terms in the thesaurus and discover which one is the preferred term. The indexers would add this term in the subject descriptors field of the database record any time the book or article was actually about that topic. So even if the author got a little creative in his or her article about the video industry and neglected to actually use the term *video* in the title or abstract, you can still find the article, because the nice indexer added the preferred term for video to the subject field of the record created to represent that article in the database.

The American Society for Indexing is a professional organization for people who index books, articles, and other information for a living. If you find yourself getting obsessed about discipline-specific thesauri and subject descriptors, perhaps you are a candidate for the indexing profession. At any rate, the ASI offers a handy list, "Online Thesauri and Authority Files," at http://www.asindexing.org/about-indexing/thesauri/online-thesauri-and -authority-files/. The thesauri that sophisticated scholarly journal databases use have a life outside those databases, and if you want to learn more about them, you can explore the ASI list. And, so you'll know, an "authority file" is an authoritative list of accepted and preferred terminology. A subject authority file lists all the agreed-on descriptors. A name authority file shows the accepted terms for individuals and organizations. A name authority file gives guidance to the indexers so they'll know, for example, whether to list the author of the book *By Any Means Necessary* as Malcolm Little or Malcolm X or El-Hajj Malik El-Shabazz, all names used by the single person who is the author of that book. Unfortunately, the ASI list is not complete. It does not include a link to the *Philosopher's Index Thesaurus*, because the publisher of that thesaurus, the Philosophy Documentation Center, wants to sell it to you for $26 instead. Nevertheless, you can check that thesaurus from within the Philosopher's Index database.

In our previous exercises, we let a quick search for obvious keywords and phrases lead us to the correct subject descriptors. But we can go straight to the thesaurus and look up terms as we plan our search strategy. Although not

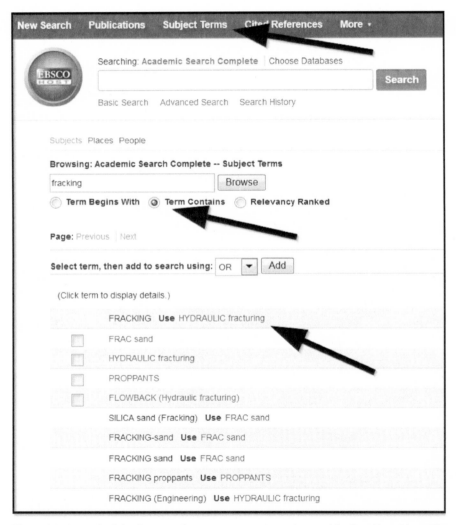

Figure 2.2. A search of the thesaurus for any term containing the word *fracking*. From MasterFile Premier. © 2015 EBSCO Industries, Inc. Used with permission of EBSCO Information Services.

every single database includes a thesaurus, you can plan your search by checking the thesaurus for descriptors to use in databases that do include them. In a database on the EBSCO platform, such as Academic Search Complete, click on the **Subject Terms** link in the blue navigation bar above the search boxes to access the thesaurus; the top arrow is pointing to it in figure 2.2. The second arrow is pointing to the option **Term Contains**, and you'll need to switch to that from the **Term Begins With** default. When you input a term in the second search box, such as *fracking* in the example, and change the button to **Term Contains**, the system searches the thesaurus (not the database) for your term, even if it's merely mentioned somewhere in the thesaurus notes. In this case, *fracking* is mentioned as the term not to use; the little word **Use** next to it means use *hydraulic fracturing* instead of fracking, because the indexing mavens have decided that *hydraulic fracturing* is the preferred term, the official descriptor, for that activity, even though most folks say "fracking." The third arrow in the figure shows how the thesaurus tells us what the correct descriptor is by instructing us to **Use** the term *hydraulic fracturing* instead of *fracking*. All of the terms in blue are approved subject descriptors; the blue terms link to more information about the word or phrase. The terms in black are natural-language keywords, not descriptors. Remember, the advantage of using descriptors is that an indexer has added them to the records representing all the items that are truly about that topic.

From the list of terms, you can click the checkbox next to the one(s) you want and then click the **Search** button next to the empty search box at the top, and the search engine will retrieve all the records in the database that have that descriptor in the subject field. No need for you to retype the descriptor into the box while you are in the thesaurus. If you ever put a keyword in a search box and limit to the subject field and get zero results, don't assume that it's because there's nothing on that topic in that database. The problem could be that your keyword is not a preferred descriptor. Check the thesaurus and try again.

FIELDS

If you have gone to the trouble of finding a preferred term, that is, a subject descriptor, then take the extra step when you input it in a search box of limiting the search to the subject field. In EBSCOhost, the field is labeled **SU** for subject. If you input a descriptor and leave the default **Find Anywhere** or **Keyword** search, you will retrieve not only the items that the indexers have tagged as being about the topic, but also any records in which the title or abstract mentions that term casually or incidentally.

The default broad keyword search is designed to bring back results, so the information seeker feels successful. Often the search system runs your broad keyword search against the subject-oriented fields only, most often the title and abstract fields. But some commercial search engines search every substantive word (not insignificant ones such as *the, in, to*), including authors' names and journal titles, so you end up with big sets of results but lots of false drops, that is, records that literally match your search query but aren't relevant to your actual research questions.

Being aware of the different fields used in a database's records can help you craft efficient searches and get more relevant results. To review, in bibliographic databases, each record represents a single item: a book, a magazine feature story, a newspaper article, an article in a scholarly journal, a paper presented at a scholarly conference, a dissertation, a technical report. And each field of the record supplies a piece of the information that you would use to cite the actual book, article, or report. Generally a complete citation to a book includes the author's name, the book's title, the place of publication, the name of the publisher, and the year published. A complete citation to an article includes the author's name, the article's title, the name of the journal or magazine in which the article appeared, the volume number (a volume usually includes one year's worth of issues), the issue information (for the individual magazine, such as the April issue or issue number 2 of four quarterly issues for the year), the year, and page numbers for the article. On the database record, the author's name goes in the author name field, and if there are two or more authors, there will be a separate field for each one. The article title goes in the article title field. The journal title goes in a separate journal title field. And so forth.

Think about an author like Stephen King. His short stories have been published widely in multiple magazines; he's the author of those stories. The wildly popular King has been written about in a lot of magazines; he's the subject of those stories. If you only want the stories he's written, you can limit your search to the author field (or, more precisely, the index of the author field). That means you won't have to wade through articles about him when all you want are the stories by him. Conversely, you can limit your search for his name to the subject field and retrieve only the records that have him listed as the subject of the article. Field searching can be powerful, so feel free to get creative. You can combine an author and journal search, for instance, to see whether or what someone has published in a particular journal. Input an author name and limit to the author field and then input a journal name and limit to the journal field. The results will include only items by that author that have been published in that journal.

You may have recently heard about a convicted felon being freed after years in prison because some new DNA testing methods showed that his DNA didn't match the DNA collected at the crime scene. And maybe you are wondering if it was a fluke or if DNA testing has been linked to other wrongful convictions. Whether you are an attorney's assistant, a member of a prison-reform group, a student majoring in criminal justice, or even a budding scientist, you might want to find research to help you understand more deeply the use of DNA testing of criminal evidence.

Let's search General OneFile's more scholarly companion database, Academic OneFile, to discover what's been published on this topic. We'll begin with a quick keyword search, but then we'll use the results to craft a much more sophisticated search with better results. The two keywords are *dna* and *innocent*, and we'll combine them with the word *and*. Figure 2.3 shows the search and the first couple of results.

There are more than two hundred results, and a lot of them use our two words, but not in the way we mean them. Quickly skimming the titles of the articles shows one near the top titled "Police Misconduct as a Cause of Wrongful Convictions." Although the article seems focused on the role of police, it does mention both of our keywords and is clearly related to the topic of criminal justice. If we click on the title, the whole article, as well as the information about the article, such as the author's name and the periodical in which it appeared, are presented.

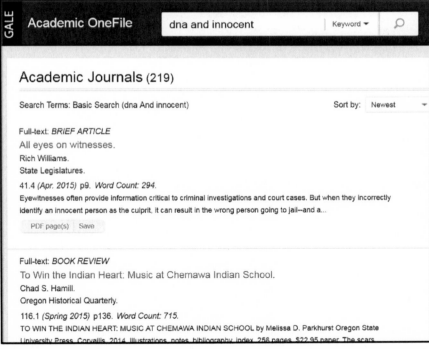

Figure 2.3. First few results from a quick search for two keywords. From Academic OneFile. © Gale, a part of Cengage Learning, Inc. Reproduced by permission www.cengage.com/permissions.

Figure 2.4. The Related Subjects box shows all of the descriptors added to this record describing an article titled "Police misconduct as a cause of wrongful convictions." From Academic One-File. © Gale, a part of Cengage Learning, Inc. Reproduced by permission www.cengage.com/permissions.

One of the most important buttons we see on the screen is labeled **Related Subjects** (see figure 2.4). Here are listed the preferred subject terms that describe what this article is about, in the opinion of the indexer who skimmed it and assigned subject terms to it. Subject terms are chosen and agreed on by experts who understand the field thoroughly. Subject terms are added to the database record describing each item indexed in the database to save you time. If you know the correct term to use is *Wrongful convictions*, then you don't have to waste time trying to think of all the words in your keyword searches authors might have used to discuss this topic. Instead of trying *falsely convicted* or *wrongfully sentenced* or *guilty when innocent*, you can simply use the preferred subject term that the experts have decided includes all those different ways of saying the same thing.

In this case, the **Related Subjects** list includes a couple of good ones for our query: *Wrongful convictions (Law)* and *DNA evidence*. Another good one is *Exoneration*. The items in the list are clickable links; if you click on *DNA evidence*, for example, you'll retrieve every item in the database that has been tagged with that subject descriptor.

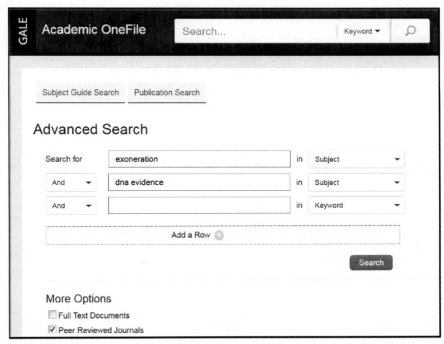

Figure 2.5. Advanced search screen showing the use of the pull-down menu to change from the default keyword to a subject search and with the option to limit to peer-reviewed journals checked. From Academic OneFile. © Gale, a part of Cengage Learning, Inc. Reproduced by permission www.cengage.com/permissions.

You don't have to drill down through the subject terms on the list, though. Once you know the preferred subject terms for your topic, you can always search directly on the advanced search screen. Since you are using the official subject terms, use the pull-down menus to the right of the search boxes to change from **Keyword** to **Subject**. Below the search boxes, check **Peer Review Journals** under the **More Options** heading to eliminate any newspaper or magazine stories, as in figure 2.5.

This search yields a couple dozen results that are about both DNA and the exoneration of individuals convicted of crimes. If we had not changed the pull-down menu to **Subject**, the search system would have retrieved almost twice as many results by including everything that mentioned those terms without being about those specific topics. Searching by **Subject** makes the database search system do the work of culling out irrelevant results for you.

The results include some full text, like the second one in figure 2.6; you can click on the **PDF page(s)** link to have immediate access to the entire article. Other results may be citations only, and you'll have to work with

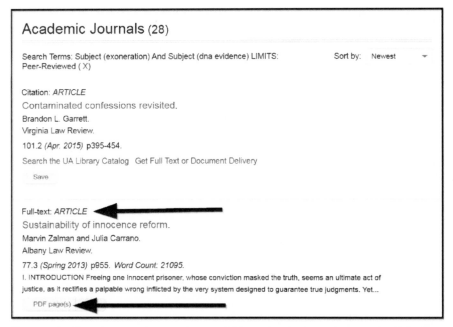

Figure 2.6. When the complete article is available in the database, the record will display a button for accessing the full text as a PDF. From Academic OneFile. © Gale, a part of Cengage Learning, Inc. Reproduced by permission www.cengage.com/permissions.

your library to get a copy of the complete article. Sometimes you want to do thorough research and know about all the publications on your topic, even if they aren't readily available in the database. Other times, you can check the little box under **More Options** and limit your results to only full text.

At every step of the search process, it's wise to assess what's happening. You may want to ask yourself if you're using the right kind of database, if your search terms are as precise as they should be, and how the search engine's features and functions can help refine your results. The first two chapters have introduced you to databases indexing general-interest and scholarly publications. Let's move on to more specialized information resources.

WHY IT WORKS

We used large databases indexing lots of scholarly sources and research articles. We identified the experts' vocabulary for our topics.
We used the experts' subject terms, listed to the left of our first result set, to drill down to the best results.
We used the advanced search screen and the pull-down menus to search by subject once we knew the preferred terms.

NOTE

1. Eric Archambault et al. *Proportion of Open-Access Peer-Reviewed Papers at the European and World Levels—2004-2011* (Montreal: Science-Metrix, 2013), http://science -metrix.com/pdf/SM_EC_OA_Availability_2004-2011.pdf.

CHAPTER 3

Is There an Opp for That?

Opportunities abound in the world of business, or so they say. Whether you are researching companies you want to work for or companies your own company is in competition with, knowing where and how to find business information can lead to a lot of opps (opportunities). Let me take you through four eye-opening exercises. The first uses Census Bureau population data to help you decide where to locate a new small business, the second provides a short guide to finding federal business opportunities, the third retrieves reports filed with the Securities and Exchange Commission (SEC) to learn more about existing companies, and the fourth uses a business-specific database to retrieve industry reports.

By the time you finish this chapter, you will be able to

- use the U.S. Census Bureau's FactFinder service to find data about neighborhood income levels,
- discover business opportunities using a U.S. government website established specifically for that purpose,
- easily identify and locate detailed financial and organizational information about publicly traded companies, and
- deploy effective search strategies in a major business database.

Suppose you've always wanted to open a luxury-goods boutique, and now you're ready to make the move. Possible locations include the affluent neighborhood around the River Oaks Country Club in Houston and the area near Lincoln Park High School in Chicago. Because a lot is riding on your decision, some research is in order. But Googling *where should I open my luxury-goods shop* isn't going to work too well. Do this instead: open a web browser window and come along as I escort you through an efficient search in an awesome resource.

Go to http://factfinder.census.gov.

Below the search box, click on **Guided Search**, then **Get Me Started**.

Leave the default button for **I'm looking for information about** people selected and click **next**.

Choose **Income/Earnings**, then **Income/Earnings (Households)**, then **next**.

Select a **Geographic Type**, then use the downward arrow in the search box to scroll down and select **5-Digit Zip Code Tabulation Area**.

In the box labeled **Select a State**, select Illinois, then scroll to the Lincoln Park zip code, *60614*, select it, and click **Add to Your Selections**.

Now change your state selection to *Texas*, scroll to the River Oaks zip code, *77019*, select it, and click **Add to Your Selections**.

Both zip codes are now in a box to the right labeled **Your Selections**. Click the *next* button.

For now, since we're interested in the entire zip code area, skip the step for race and ethnicity information by again clicking the *next* button.

Click the link labeled *Income in the Past 12 Months*.

Results! When the table of numeric data appears on your screen, take a breath. Then read the column headings. You'll see that the data in the left-hand columns include the number of households, families, and married-couple families for the Lincoln Park neighborhood. The right-hand columns have the comparable data for the River Oaks area. As you look through the rows of information giving the number of households and families, you'll see the percentage of each with annual income ranging from less than $10,000 to more than $200,000. Below those income ranges, you'll see a row for income medians and a row for income means for the different groupings of people. Bottom line: there are more households and families in the Chicago zip code, which may mean more customers, but the Houstonians are richer, which may mean more actual spending at your boutique.

As with many kinds of research, new knowledge leads to new questions. But at least you have some hard figures to include in your decision-making process.

Let's suppose you have a different kind of company, say, not retail, but a consulting firm of some sort. You're not looking for a location; you're looking for contracts. The federal government outsources quite a bit of work to established firms, and as you might suspect, there's a system for becoming one of those firms with lucrative government contracts. All the information you need is gathered and presented at a single website: FedBizOpps.gov, https://www.fbo.gov/. The site functions as a marketplace, in the sense that government agencies can announce opportunities on it, registered vendors can identify and bid on opportunities, and government representatives can review vendor profiles and proposals. You don't have to register to view general information about the website, read news about opportunities, browse opportunities, and check lists of agencies. Not all listings are actual opportunities for contracts; some involve an agency's attempt to collect preliminary information before issuing a solicitation for bids. The website provides tutorials, including instructional videos, to help you learn how to register and use the service.

Browsing opportunities shows the kinds of goods and services the federal government solicits bids for, as well as the requirements and deadlines for bids. After the deadline has passed and the decision has been made, the name of the company that won the bid will be added to the list, which can be helpful if you are interested in tracking the success of your competitors. Figure 3.1 shows three recent opportunities listed on FedBizOpps.gov: an Army request for proposals for septic tank pumping, a Department of Health and Human Services need for someone to maintain one of its microscopes, and a Department of Agriculture research station's search for a company to replace a structure's screening.

As figure 3.2 shows, the home page offers a series of search boxes with pull-down menus that let you filter results in a variety of ways, such as the **Set-Aside Code** pull-down that lets you select opportunities for women-owned businesses or the **Place of Performance** menu for limiting to opportunities that require you to travel to Hawaii to do the work (hey, somebody's got to do it!).

Some of the biggest U.S. companies have thrived on such government contracts, but plenty of companies have made their fortunes from consumers like us. For our next exercise, we'll check out a well-known company to assess its fiscal health and see what it views as its threats and opportunities. Companies that sell their stock on one of the major U.S. stock exchanges

Ql **S--Eau Galle Project Sanitary Pumping Services** W912ES15T0063 S -- Utilities and housekeeping services	**Department of the Army** U.S. Army Corps of Engineers USACE District, St. Paul
Ql **Service contract for the maintenance of Leica SP5 Miscroscope** HHS-NIH-NIDA-SSSA-SBSS-2015-406 J -- Maintenance, repair & rebuilding of equipment	**Department of Health and Human Services** National Institutes of Health National Institute on Drug Abuse, Station Support/Simplified Acquisitions
Ql **Rescreen existing screenhouse** AG-32SD-S-15-0005 Z -- Maintenance, repair, and alteration of real property	**Department of Agriculture** Agricultural Research Service Western Business Service Center

Figure 3.1. Three opportunities listed on FedBizOpps.gov.

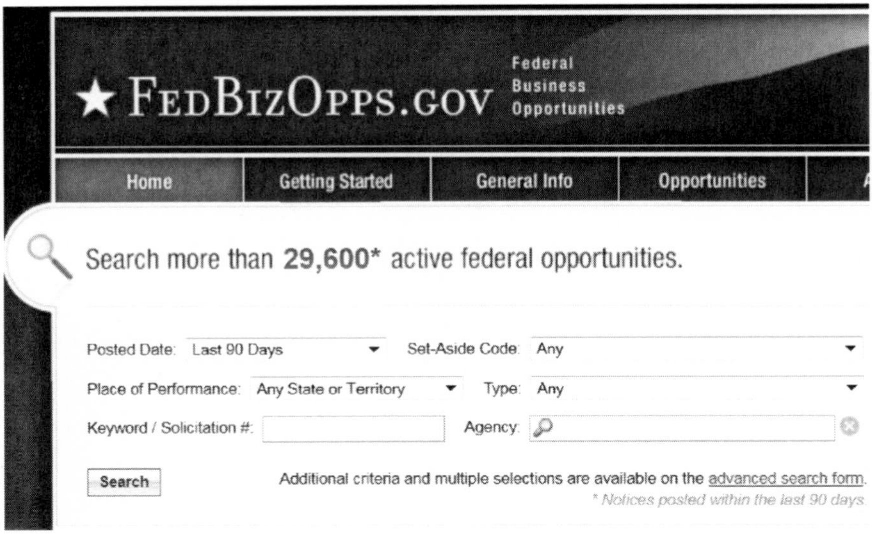

Figure 3.2. FedBizOpps.gov search screen with pull-down menus for options such as place of performance and set-aside code.

are public (as opposed to private) companies. A federal government agency, the SEC, requires each public company to submit a full disclosure of financial and other data each year. These full annual reports are referred to as 10-Ks, and submitting them is referred to as "filing." The SEC uses a "ticker symbol" for each company, and we can think of those as the company's nickname. For example, Southwest Airlines has the ticker symbol LUV, and Molson Coors Brewing is TAP. Not all ticker symbols are so clever. Apple's is plain old AAPL. People who buy and sell stocks like to look at 10-Ks (as well as quarterly and other filings) to learn more about the companies they are investing in. Job seekers can learn a lot about a company where they might like to work. And business researchers can use different company reports to compare performance and to get a sense of how an entire industry is doing.

In the SEC's EDGAR database of public company filings, it's a lot easier to use the ticker symbol to search, if you know it, but you can search by company name instead, as shown in figure 3.3.

Start at http://www.sec.gov/.
In the blue navigation bar, click on **Filings/Company Filings Search**.
In the **Fast Search** box, input the ticker symbol LUV.
The results are lots of different filings; scroll down to the 10-K that Southwest Airlines submitted to the SEC in February 2014, and click on the **Documents** choice.
Choose Form 10-K, luv-12312013x10k.htm.

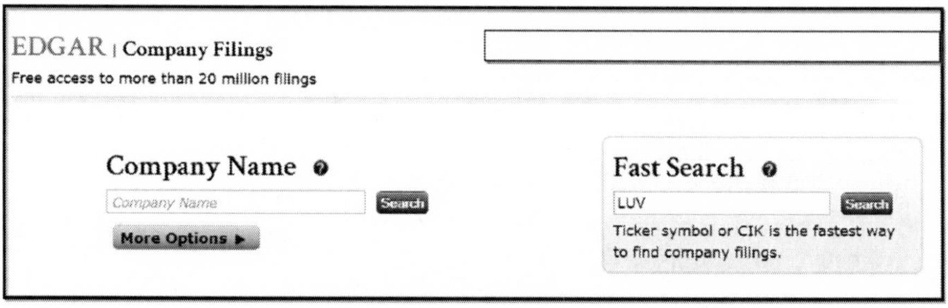

Figure 3.3. EDGAR company filings database with the ticker symbol for Southwest Airlines in the fast search box.

Take some time to skim through the whole thing. Your eyes might glaze over when it comes to some of the business and government jargon, but there's some interesting stuff here, too. The 10-K begins with an overview of the business and the risks it faces. Not surprisingly, the cost of fuel and the need to replace old jets are on the minds of Southwest's executives. Keep going, and you'll find charts and tables showing how shares are doing (should we buy?), the total amount (in millions) of cash the company holds, revenues, and other financial data.

Perhaps one of your former teachers convinced you that any website with .com at the end of its URL was suspect. In fact, a company can be one of the most authoritative sources about itself. Many publicly traded companies now provide the exact same 10-Ks and other SEC-required reports not only on the EDGAR database but also on their own websites. If you are tracking one or a few companies, you may want to forgo EDGAR in favor of going directly to the company website, where there will most likely be a link for investors and then a link for filings.

As you may have guessed by now, the U.S. federal government is one of the largest publishers of information in the world. And by law, all published information created by federal government employees as part of their job responsibilities and at taxpayers' expense is in the public domain. That means there's no charge to access it directly from a government website. There are exceptions, of course; for national security reasons, some government information is kept secret. But the amount and kind of information and data you can find for free at U.S. government websites are jaw-dropping.

Of course, commercial enterprises collect, organize, and make available company, industry, and product information as well, often for a fee. Magazine and newspaper articles are great sources of business information. The *New York Times*, *Los Angeles Times*, and *Wall Street Journal* are major newspapers covering business, and most newspapers cover local business developments. Newspapers offer online editions that you can browse and search for articles about local business executives, companies, industries, and products, as well as learning about the city itself as a setting for business activity. One important business database is ABI/Inform, which indexes major magazines and newspapers, including the *Wall Street Journal*.

You can do the same kinds of searches you would do in any other database. Using the name of a business or business owner as keywords, for example, will find any news or feature stories that mention that firm or person. But business databases may offer additional kinds of content quite different from newspaper and magazine articles. Here's one concrete example: ABI/Inform indexes market reports, industry data, annual reports, and other kinds of material not indexed in many other kinds of databases. Above the search boxes on the advanced search screen is a link to **Data & Reports** that can limit your results to useful material. Perhaps I am interested in understanding what's happening with the domestic farm-raised catfish industry. Figure 3.4 is a screenshot of a search on the Data & Reports screen, which I've limited further by checking the **Industry Reports** box.

I received 88 results and discovered that there are quarterly updates about the aquaculture industry, of which catfish is a part, and the latest one is only a few days old. Included are cool graphics to help the reader visualize the data presented, as seen in figure 3.5. Among all of you reading this book, I'm betting no more than nine care about catfish farming. But if you end up working for a company that's trying to break into the aquaculture industry or needing a detailed report on any industry, think how smart you'll look when you turn up goodies like this!

Should you venture into your local university or public library to track down business information, you might find that your thoughtful and com-

Figure 3.4. Data & Reports Search screen, with the search for *catfish* limited to industry reports. Source: ABI/Inform Complete, ProQuest LLC.

The output of US animal production (except cattle and poultry and eggs), which includes aquaculture, is forecast to grow at an annual compounded rate of 5 percent between 2014 and 2018. Data Published: September 2014

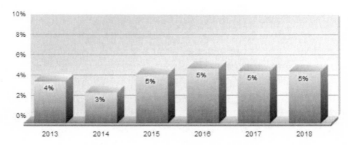

Figure 3.5. Example of a table from a report on the aquaculture industry. Source: First Research Industry Profiles, Aquaculture—Quarterly Update 7/28/2014, Austin, TX: Dun & Bradstreet, 2014, [4]. Used with permission by Dun & Bradstreet, 2015.

passionate librarians, bless their hearts, have made a list of databases by subject. So even if you've forgotten to take this book along, you can easily steer yourself to the right tools for finding articles and reports related to business. And of course, the list of databases by subject will be on the library's website, too. Figure 3.6 shows an example from a university library.

Databases by Subject: Business

Business	▾

ABI/Inform Complete (1971-)
Access to articles, summaries and citations from over 3000 management, marketing, and general business periodicals from 1971 to the present.

Access Business News
Access to business and law journals, local and regional business news weeklies and other news sources across North America. 1980-present

BCC Research
Market research that focuses on high-tech markets. Areas focus include advanced materials, advanced transportation technologies, biotechnology, chemicals, energy and resources, engineering, environment, food and beverage, fuel cell and battery technologies, healthcare, information technology, instrumentation and sensors manufacturing, membrane and separation technology, nanotechnology, pharmaceuticals, plastics, safety and security, semiconductor manufacturing.

Business Insights: Essentials
Company and industry profiles, company brand information, business rankings, investment reports, and articles from business periodicals; coverage starts 1976 (varies by publication)

Business Source Complete
Citations to articles in more than 1,300 business journals plus detailed author profiles for the 40,000 most-cited authors. Coverage starts in 1965.

EconLit
Citations with some abstracts of literature in economics from journals, essays, proceedings, books, book reviews, dissertations, and working papers. 1969-present.

Figure 3.6. An academic library's list of databases by subject, for business. Courtesy University of Arizona Libraries. © Arizona Board of Regents for the University of Arizona.

Subject-oriented lists may be confined to the commercial databases that a library pays for and thus wants to promote to its users. Government resources may not be intertwined with commercial resources in such lists. Nevertheless, a combination of resources will almost always provide a more thorough and balanced picture of a company or industry than the use of a single database or website can. So, if you are looking at a list of databases by subject, you might skim the government category along with the business category.

WHY IT WORKS

We visited specific federal government websites to search for specific kinds of information.

We learned some insider tricks such as the use of ticker-symbol searching for quick retrieval of company information.

We realized that a commercial database devoted to the subject of business can be a great source of articles from trade journals and other periodicals as well as for specialized reports on industries.

Good point: Using both government and commercial resources can yield a profitable mix of information.

CHAPTER 4

Dazzle Them with Statistics

Sometimes you need a number to make your case. You need statistics, data, figures. Or maybe someone is trying to make a case to you (listening to talk radio again, are we?), and you want to chase down that digit he or she mentioned. Statistics are out there: about people, the economy, health, our physical world. We'll take each one in turn.

By the time you finish this chapter, you will be able to

- use two different strategies to find U.S. Census data about populations and their characteristics,
- discover information about American industries from the Economic Census,
- find numeric data from a wide range of sources by using a commercial database of statistics, and
- browse through alphabetized topics on a U.S. government website to locate statistical information on a variety of subjects.

The U.S. Census Bureau stays busy year-round slicing and dicing data about us. It serves up this data on a big platter called American FactFinder, and what could be tastier than a free smorgasbord of facts? But let's not forget we're dealing with the feds here, and things might get a little complicated. That's why the home page gives you four main options for finding figures: a search box, a guided search, an advanced search, and a download center. The best for newbies are the search box and the guided search. We'll practice using both.

Start at American FactFinder, http://factfinder.census.gov/.
Input *Bend, Oregon* in the search box and hit **Go**.

Figure 4.1 shows the result screen for this search.

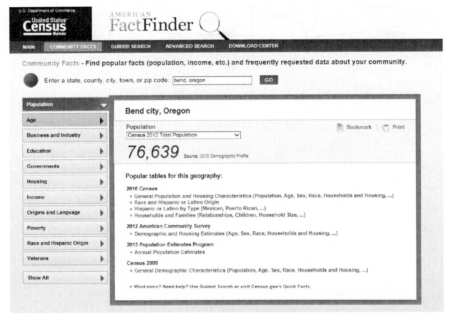

Figure 4.1. Data for the city of Bend, Oregon, available from the U.S. Census Bureau's American FactFinder website.

The population at the last census is shown in big blue numbers, and more details on different aspects of this city are available in the blue links below the total population figure and from the blue tabs in the left-hand menu. Figure 4.2 shows what happens if you click on the left-side **Education** tab.

Depending on the information you need, you can click through the various links to find all kinds of information about our friends in Bend. Notice the enticing little "Want more? Need help?" at the bottom of the white box, along with the suggestion to try the Guided Search. Let's take that suggestion now.

Start at the **Guided Search** page, http://factfinder2.census.gov/faces/nav/jsf/pages/guided_search.xhtml, as shown in figure 4.3.

The numbered blue tabs across the top walk you through options. For example, the first step is to choose a topic, and the choices include people, housing, business or industry, or a specific data set or table you already know about. You can choose options on a series of screens and eventually end up with a set of results in the form of tables of numbers. We'll leave the first button on **I'm looking for information about** people and click the **next** button on the bottom right of the screen.

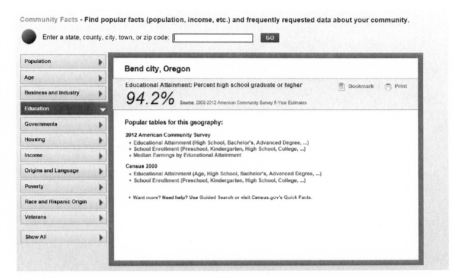

Figure 4.2. Data for the city of Bend, Oregon, available from the U.S. Census Bureau's American FactFinder website.

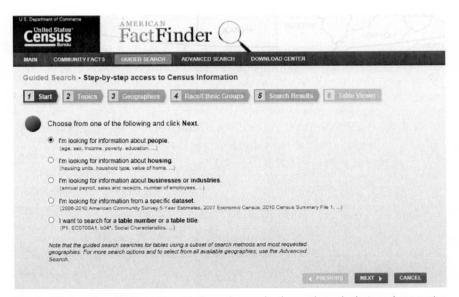

Figure 4.3. American FactFinder's guided search page leads you through choices about topics, geographies, and racial/ethnic groups.

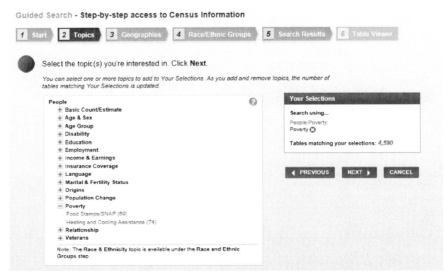

Figure 4.4. Choices of topics in American FactFinder's guided search.

On the **Topics** screen, we'll click on **Poverty** to see our choices, then click on **Poverty** again (instead of the other two choices, involving food stamps and heating/cooling assistance). As shown in figure 4.4, the little box to the right keeps track of what we've selected so far—People/Poverty—and a whopping 4,590 Census data tables have statistics about that. (When you try it, the number may be larger still.)

We haven't chosen a place yet, so click on the next button again to go to the **Geography** screen. We have a choice of entering a place-name or zip code in the search box or of using the pull-down menu to select a geographic area, such as a state or several states. For now, let's input Oregon in the search box and click **Go**. We can choose a county or counties, or we can stick with the state overall. We'll go with Deschutes County, home to lovely Bend, Oregon. The next button takes us to the **Race/Ethnic Groups** page, where we can choose from among several categories that the U.S. government uses when it sends out census questionnaires. Click on **Select from Basic Groups** and choose **American Indian**, then click the next button. We're down to 107 tables (see figure 4.5), and they are listed for us with a bit of information in the right-hand column about where the data come from. For example, the first table listed is from the 2013 American Community Survey (ACS), which the Census Bureau uses to update the ten-year census by sampling smaller numbers of people and estimating population based on those samples. Clicking on the first table listed reveals detailed information about the poverty level of American

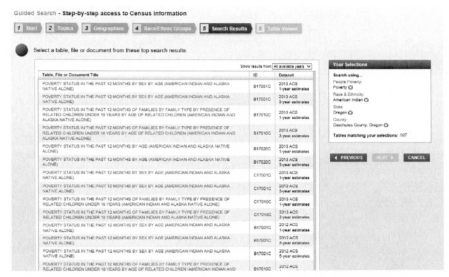

Figure 4.5. Results of an American FactFinder guided search for data about poverty among Native American residents of Oregon's Deschutes County.

Indians living in Deschutes County, including age breakdowns that tell us how many are under the age of five, over the age of seventy-four, and several ranges in between.

Everyone knows that the U.S. Census Bureau tallies us all up every ten years in the decennial census. You may not know that the bureau tallies up business establishments every five years in a data-gathering frenzy called the Economic Census. Business establishments complete a questionnaire about their revenues, number of employees, and other information, and the federal government supplements the returned questionnaires with data from business tax returns and other sources. Then the government outputs the data in a series over time. By the time some of the data is released for public consumption, it's a bit out of date and the next Economic Census is gearing up, but the availability of the same data in five-year snapshots over many years can reveal a lot about the U.S. economy and individual industries, even small mom-and-pop-oriented ones like tortilla manufacturing.

Start at the U.S. Census Bureau, http://www.census.gov/en.html.

We'll browse to begin.

Click on the **Topics** tab in the blue navigation bar and select **Business**.

Under the heading "The Economic Census," click on **2012 Economic Census**.

In the box labeled "Industry & Local Business Statistics," click on the **See economic statistics** link. You may have to scroll down to find it.
Then click on the **View an Industry Snapshot** link.

The U.S. economy is divided into eighteen sectors, and each sector has a code number, shown to the left of the name of the sector. For example, the manufacturing sector uses the codes 31–33, while the health care and social assistance sector of the economy uses the code 62. These codes are also assigned in Canada and Mexico, as part of the North American Industry Classification System (NAICS). Skim the list of industries on the left of the screen; choose one, let's say 62; and click on it to see a table presenting statistics for that industry, plus a map for quickly visualizing which states have the most economic activity in that sector. You may want to use the pull-down menu to change the map to show different statistics about the industry.

Here's a crucial thing to understand when you look at a table of statistics. The column and/or row headings in the table will tell you how to understand the figures given. In the table for sector 62, for example, the row showing annual payroll has the notation **($ Millions)**, meaning the figures are dollars and in millions. So you need to multiply the figure shown for annual payroll by 1,000,000; in other words, add six zeroes to the figure given. If you don't pay attention to this, you can make an obvious error (and believe me, lots of students do!). You may report that the total annual payroll (the amount of money paid to employees working in this sector) was $804,364, as reported in the 2012 Economic Census. But look at the next row down. Total employment was 18,587,467. Simple division suggests there's something wrong here. Do we believe that more than eighteen million people earned only a total of $804,364? Makes a lot more sense that eighteen million people earned a total of $804,364,000,000, doesn't it? That's on average a bit less than $68,000 annual salary, which sounds about right. Keep an eye on those pesky column and row headings, especially when you are interpreting numbers.

Check out the data for another economic sector, perhaps one you are interested in working in. If you click on the little symbol to the left of the industry name instead of clicking on the industry name, a menu will open showing you finer and finer subsets of that industry. If you are only interested in the hospital industry, you can click on the symbol next to sector 62 and then double-click on subsector 622 Hospitals to see the table of statistics and the map.

All levels of government and government-like entities gather statistics, from individual states to the United Nations and European Union. Statistical Insight, a database that indexes hundreds of thousands of tables and publications and provides full text for many, is available at some university

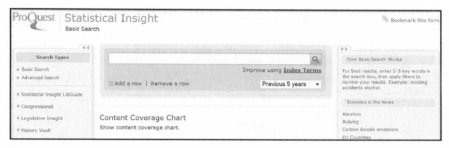

Figure 4.6. Basic search screen for a numeric database. Source: Statistical Insight, ProQuest LLC.

and college libraries. It's available from the database vendor ProQuest, a competitor of Gale and EBSCO, with its own platform and search engine. It offers basic and advanced search screens, but you may as well begin with the basic screen, where you can input a few keywords or check the thesaurus for descriptors (which ProQuest calls "index terms") and limit to the latest two, five, or ten years, or retrieve material going as far back as the statistics for your topic are available. To the right of the search screen, as shown in figure 4.6, is an alphabetical list of hot topics that you can browse to find statistics related to each.

If your topic isn't listed in the **Statistics in the News** list of hot topics, you can browse the index terms and submit your search from there. In figure 4.7, I have clicked on the **Index Terms** link on the basic search page, then

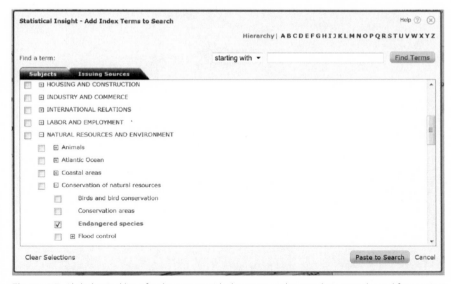

Figure 4.7. Alphabetical list of index terms with the topic *endangered species* selected for pasting into the search box. Source: Statistical Insight, ProQuest LLC.

scrolled down to the broad category *Natural Resources and Environment* and
clicked on the plus sign next to that category to view subcategories. Under
the subcategory *Conservation of natural resources*, I have checked the box for
endangered species. When I hit the **Paste to Search** button, in the lower right
of the screen, that term will be automatically entered in the search box back
on the basic search screen, and I can click on the little **magnifying glass
icon** to the right of the search box to activate the retrieval of results that
have been tagged with that index term.

The results screen lets you limit in several different ways, as shown in
figure 4.8. In the left-side menu are time period sliders that let you specify a range of dates for the statistics themselves or for the years when the
reports and tables were published. Under the sliders are filters for **Source**
of the statistics, where you can choose to view only data compiled by international organizations such as the United Nations or only data from U.S.
federal agencies or commercial publishers. Additional filters for geographic
regions, further subcategories of data, and subject descriptors are provided.

The results screen in Statistical Insight lets you limit to full statistical
reports or to stand-alone numeric tables. The top arrow in figure 4.8 shows
the tab for limiting results to the full text of reports in PDF format, and the
bottom arrow points to an example of such a report. The top circle shows

Figure 4.8. Results screen for *endangered species* index term search, with results limited to the
last five years. Source: Statistical Insight, ProQuest LLC.

the tab for limiting results to tables of data, and the second circle indicates an example of such a table. If you click on the **Table** button for one of the results, you will see the complete table of data, and you may be offered the option of downloading a PDF or a spreadsheet of the data to your computer.

Because Statistical Insight is a highly specialized database, only some academic libraries will buy access to it. If you live near a university or college library that subscribes to it, you may have to visit the physical library or pay the library for remote access to the database. ProQuest does not sell access directly to individuals. However, the main advantage of the database is that it offers a one-stop shop for all kinds of statistical information. If you understand that many governments collect statistics and post them freely on the Internet, you can use your favorite web search engine to find a lot of data. Even better, start at the web portal of the U.S. government devoted to numbers, USA.gov's Data and Statistics page, at http://www.usa.gov/Topics/Reference-Shelf/Data.shtml, shown in figure 4.9.

On the USA.gov Data and Statistics page, you can browse topics in alphabetical order, drilling down through subtopics to find the information you need. On the left side of the screen is a link to a service called **Ask a Government Information Librarian**, where you can use a chat room or e-mail to get professional assistance with locating the statistics you need. A link beneath the Data and Statistics heading takes you to the Data.gov website to search for numeric information. Data.gov is designed for people who are sharing data sets and using sophisticated tools for analyzing sta-

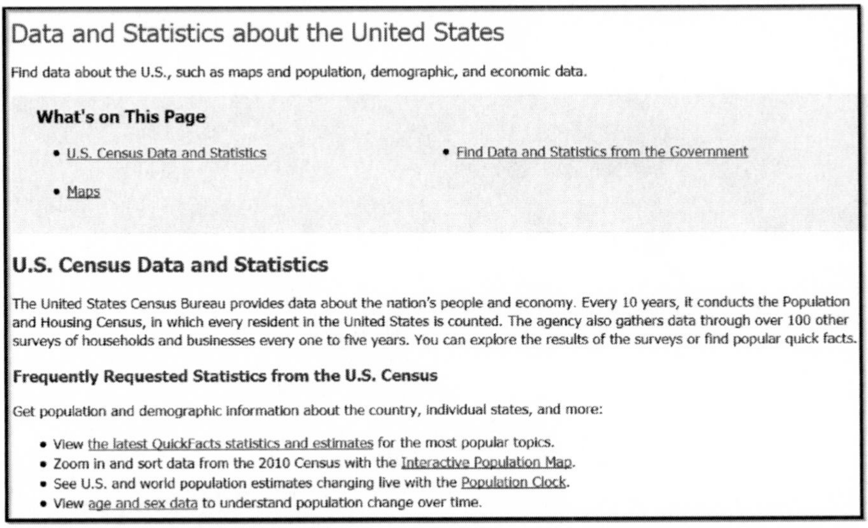

Data and Statistics about the United States

Find data about the U.S., such as maps and population, demographic, and economic data.

What's on This Page

- U.S. Census Data and Statistics
- Maps
- Find Data and Statistics from the Government

U.S. Census Data and Statistics

The United States Census Bureau provides data about the nation's people and economy. Every 10 years, it conducts the Population and Housing Census, in which every resident in the United States is counted. The agency also gathers data through over 100 other surveys of households and businesses every one to five years. You can explore the results of the surveys or find popular quick facts.

Frequently Requested Statistics from the U.S. Census

Get population and demographic information about the country, individual states, and more:

- View the latest QuickFacts statistics and estimates for the most popular topics.
- Zoom in and sort data from the 2010 Census with the Interactive Population Map.
- See U.S. and world population estimates changing live with the Population Clock.
- View age and sex data to understand population change over time.

Figure 4.9. USA.gov's data and statistics page.

tistics, rather than for the student who needs some numbers to enhance a term paper or a business owner who wants some figures that will help gauge markets, estimate the tax burden in different locations, or quantify the size of an industry. If you want data you can slice, dice, and crunch, by all means visit Data.gov. But for most everyday uses of statistics, the USA.gov Data and Statistics page is a great place to start.

WHY IT WORKS

To find freely available statistics, we visited a federal government agency, the Census Bureau, known for counting people and things.

We learned about a commercial database that indexes huge amounts of statistical reports and tables.

We also learned there might be alternative routes to finding statistics and data besides relying exclusively on a commercial index available in only some libraries.

Good point: Thinking carefully about the level of involvement you want to have with numbers can help you decide whether to find statistics you can cite or data you can use with statistical analysis software.

CHAPTER 5

Doing Good, Searching Well

Not-for-profit organizations do a lot of good in the world, and so do the many individuals who support them. Whether you are researching nonprofits as a potential donor or a potential recipient of help or as an employee of a charitable organization prospecting for donors, knowing where and how to find information can make your work easier while you make the world a better place.

By the time you finish this chapter, you will be able to

- find information about nonprofit organizations by using a website dedicated to assessing charitable organizations,
- research grant-making organizations and grant opportunities, and
- learn more about individuals who give to charities by finding articles about them in news databases and biographical resources.

A pet-loving friend of mine has been looking for a charity to give a few dollars to every month. She's heard some horror stories about charities that spend a lot of their donations on keeping the staff rather than the clients happy, so she'd like some reassurance that her money is being put to good use. A friend of hers donates to a place in Utah called "Best Friends." Let's help my friend find out more information before she parts with any cash.

Go to Charity Navigator at http://www.charitynavigator.org/.
In the search box near the top of the home page, input *best friends*, then click the blue search button.

With only a few results, ours is the first on the list, Best Friends Animal Society in Kanab, Utah, with three out of a possible four stars. Clicking the name of the organization takes you to Charity Navigator's detailed assessment of Best Friends Animal Society, including a few charts and graphs, and toward the bottom of the page, a list of similar organizations that the Navigator deems "highly rated." Think of it as a shopping tool for your philanthropic spending.

Most of the data the Navigator uses for its rating system come from federal tax forms, specifically Form 990, which 501(c)(3) charities file annually. The 501(c)(3) designation is granted by the federal government and means that any donation you give to such an organization is tax-deductible. Not all philanthropic organizations are included in Charity Navigator's ratings, so you may want to use the blue navigation bar at the top of the home page to visit the Methodology page for an explanation of who's in and who's out.

By clicking on the **Advanced** link in the blue navigation bar, you can access Charity Navigator's advanced search screen, as shown in figure 5.1. It includes a pull-down menu for selecting the cause(s) the charity supports, such as animal welfare, environmental activism, and health issues. More fields, including salary ranges for CEOs of charitable organizations, are available for searching if you register at the site. To the left of the advanced search form is a menu for browsing a directory of the site; a list of all the top-rated, four-star charities; and additional information.

Charity Navigator waits until seven yearly tax forms have been filed before compiling the data and issuing a rating. So we'll need to look elsewhere for newbies. Let's check with the Internal Revenue Service (IRS) to see whether our donations to a new organization we've heard of, Paws and Affection, located near Philadelphia, will be tax deductible.

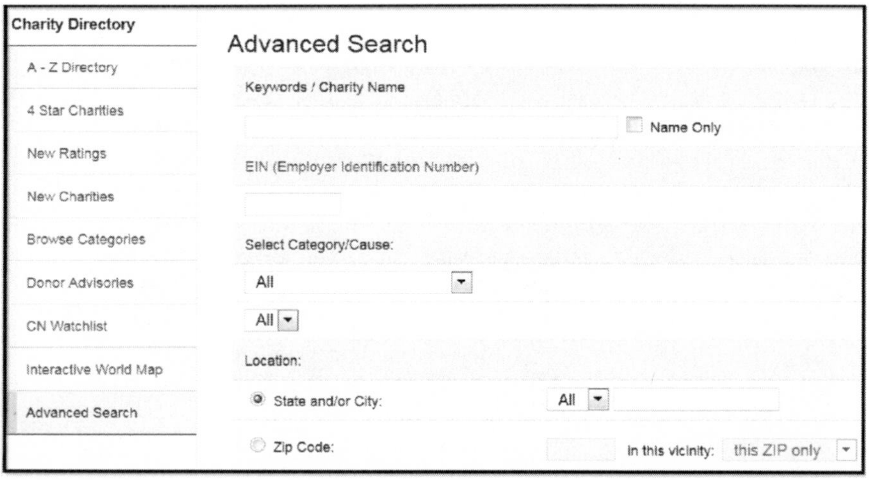

Figure 5.1. Charity Navigator's advanced search form, with options for browsing listed in the menu to the left. Used with permission of Charity Navigator.

Go to the IRS Exempt Organizations Select Check database at http://www
.irs.gov/Charities-&-Non-Profits/Exempt-Organizations-Select-Check.

You may want to skim the information on that page and then click the
blue button that takes you to the search tool.

You'll have three options for limiting your results, to charities that can
receive tax-deductible contributions, charities that no long have the
right to accept tax-deductible donations, and charities that bring in so
little money that they are allowed to file an abbreviated Form 990-N.
Choose the first option, and a search form appears.

In the name box, type "paws and affection" and do include the quotation
marks so the system will read it as a phrase rather than as unrelated
keywords.

Use the State pull-down menu to select Pennsylvania.

With such a distinctive name, it's not surprising that the one and only
Paws and Affection, Inc., is our one and only result. The last tidbit of information, to the far right of the screen, indicates this organization is "PC."
It's a public charity, meaning we can give up to half of our adjusted gross
income to it (with a few stipulations) should we no longer have the need to
spend our income on, say, food or rent. For quick reassurance that you can
legally deduct your charitable donation on your federal income tax form,
use the IRS Exempt Organizations database.

GRANT SEEKING

Another great database comes from the Foundation Center, an outfit that
publishes information about organizations that provide monetary grants to
worthy projects. If you or your organization is seeking grants, this should be
one of your first resources. The Foundation Center keeps its database, the
Foundation Directory Online, on a tight leash. It is not accessible for free on
the web. You can pay to subscribe via the web, and that may be worthwhile
if you are using the database a lot. For free (to you) access, you have to make
a visit to one of the institutions in the Funding Information Network, such
as your local public library. A directory of Funding Information Network
institutions is at http://foundationcenter.org/fin/. A lot of the libraries in
the network host workshops where you can learn how to search the *Foundation Directory Online*. Limited searching of the *Foundation Directory Online*
is available for free if you register at the GrantSpace website, hosted by the
Foundation Center at http://grantspace.org/.

At no charge, you can search by grant maker name or its Employer Iden-
tification Number (EIN) if you are already familiar with a philanthropic
organization and need more information, or you can search by location if

you want a list of grant makers in your town and some basic information about them. Other strategies, such as searching for granting organizations by the kinds of activities they support or by using keywords, are not possible without a paid subscription. The GrantSpace site provides grant-writing and related training for free online and a searchable knowledge base that can answer frequently asked questions.

The U.S. government gives grants to organizations and groups, but generally not to individuals. A quick hands-on exercise will demonstrate the kinds of federal grants available.

Navigate to http://grants.gov. The section labeled **Find Open Grant Opportunities** gives some options for filtering programs currently accepting grant applications (see figure 5.2). Select the tab **Browse Eligibilities** to see grants for specific groups, including nonprofit organizations with and without the 501(c)(3) designation.

Click on the link for **Nonprofits having a 501(c)(3) status with the IRS** to see more than nine hundred offerings. The column on the left presents checkboxes you can use to filter results by type of funding, eligibility for the program, subject categories, and government agencies.

The search box above the column lets you search by keyword. If you use the search box, it searches the entire database, wiping out any filters you may have checked off when you were browsing by eligibility. As with most

Figure 5.2. The feature labeled Find Open Grant Opportunities on the GRANTS.gov website makes it possible to browse categories of government grant-making agencies.

search boxes, putting phrases in quotation marks will bring back results for the phrase and not for all the items mentioning both words anywhere they appear, so you'll have fewer and better results to look through. But searching by phrase can leave out some important results because they don't happen to mention your phrase. Let's see how this works when we look for grant opportunities for our nonprofit group dedicated to restoring native plants to the rural landscape.

In the search box, input *"native plant restoration"* including the quotation marks. Hit the **Search** button to make the system go. You'll get one or at most a few results.

Now try the search without the quotation marks. You'll have more than one hundred results. From there, you can use some of the checkboxes to filter further. As you can see in figure 5.3, I've filtered so only grant opportunities are in the results.

The results are displayed to the right of the search form. You can click on the funding opportunity number to read more about each grant program and how to apply.

PROSPECTING

Philanthropy runs on individual donations. In 2013, according to *Giving USA*, Americans gave more than $300 billion dollars to charities, about 72 percent of total charitable donations for the year. Lots of those dollars from individuals and families arrived in small chunks in response to broad appeals for support.[1] If you want to identify individuals and families who have more to give and then turn them from prospective donors into actual donors, you should start by doing some prospect research. By reading your local daily and weekly newspapers and monthly magazines, you probably already know the wealthiest and the most philanthropic folks in your town. You see their names in the business news and on the society pages, where they may be pictured at fund-raising events such as auctions, dinners, benefit concerts, and charity balls. As with everything else, you can Google them to find out more. But there are more productive ways to sleuth.

One of the best is to search popular newspaper and magazine indexes using people's names as the keywords and phrases. By selecting a database that indexes local and regional newspapers and magazines, you increase your chances of finding material about local heroes and angels.

For example, the General OneFile database indexes seven publications related to the city of Houston, Texas. How do I know? I accessed the database via my local library, so I would not have to pay a fee, clicked on the **Publication Search** link, and input *houston* in the publications search box, as shown in figure 5.4. As in most search engines, you don't need to capitalize proper names.

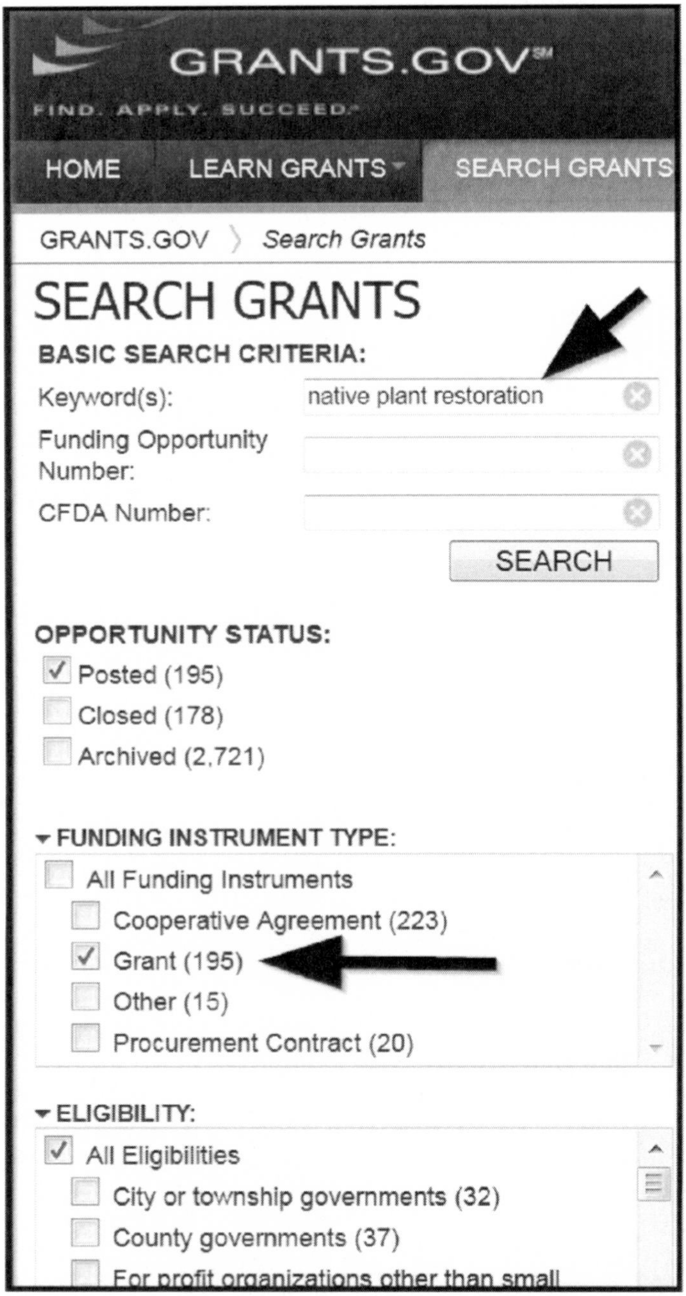

Figure 5.3. Advanced search form available at the Search Grants tab on Grants.gov. Results for a keyword search for *native plant restoration*, filtered for grants only, total 195 listings.

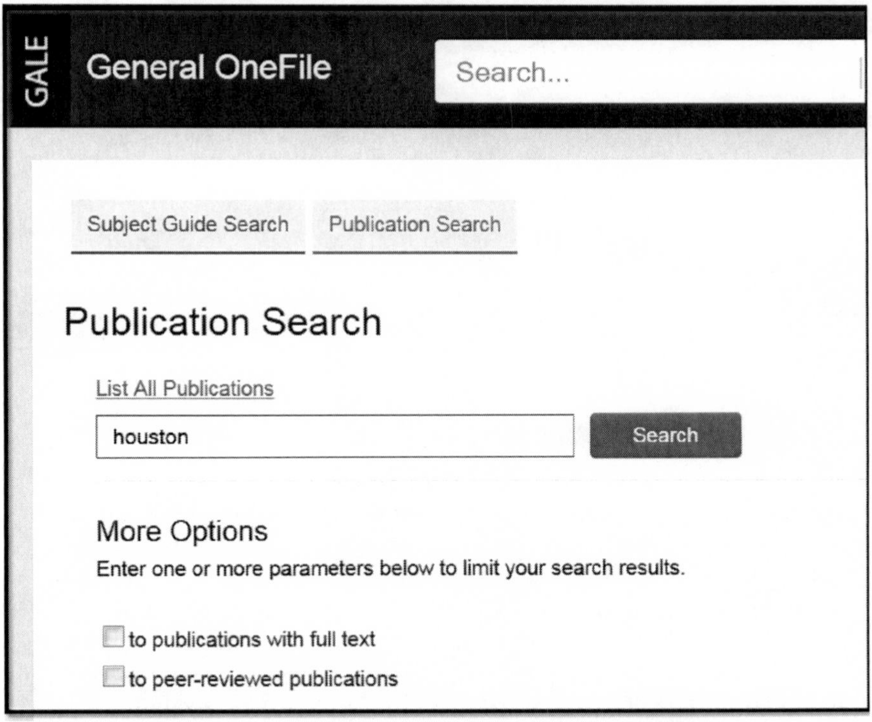

Figure 5.4. Example of a publication search. From General OneFile. © Gale, a part of Cengage Learning, Inc. Reproduced by permission www.cengage.com/permissions.

The seven results for Houston include a major daily newspaper, *The Houston Chronicle*. You can search the *Chronicle*'s archives on the paper's website, but if you want the full text of an article you find there, you will have to pay for it. If you use General OneFile via your local library instead, you'll have free access to the full text of articles from the newspaper because your library subscribes. General OneFile indexes legal and business periodicals published in and/or focused on Houston, as well as a travel guide to the city published by Fodor's. We used a city name, but you can search for states; the General OneFile database indexes thirteen Arizona publications.

When you conduct a publication search in General OneFile, your results simply list the publications indexed in the database, along with some basic information about each publication. To actually search for content in those publications, use the advanced search form. In this case, we are prospecting for philanthropists, wealthy and successful individuals in our city or state who are known for giving back to their communities. So in the advanced search form, input an individual's name in one search box, then in the next

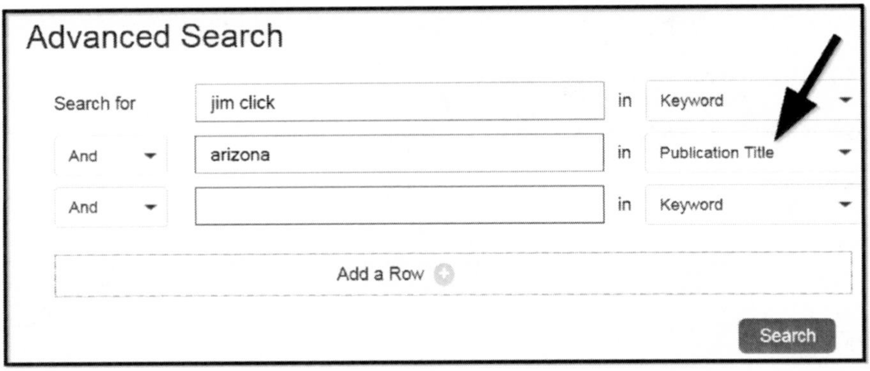

Figure 5.5. Advanced Search form, showing a search for an individual in any publication indexed in this database and having *arizona* in its name. From General OneFile. © Gale, a part of Cengage Learning, Inc. Reproduced by permission www.cengage.com/permissions.

search box input a city or state name and use the pull-down menu to limit the search to the field labeled **Publication Title**, as shown in figure 5.5.

Let's think about this strategy for a minute. If we left the search on the default, keyword anywhere, we'd retrieve records for articles published in any publication indexed by the database that mentions our prospect and our city or state. Since most articles will mention where a person lives as a way to identify the person, we could retrieve a lot of articles that don't serve our purpose, which is to find out what local activities the person is involved in. Local periodicals and newspapers are more likely to cover that kind of thing. When we use the pull-down menu to limit to **Publication Title**, the search engine will look anywhere in the title for the word we input—we don't have to give the entire title. If you want to limit your results to one single title, you can, by typing in the title of the publication instead of the city or state name and, again, using the pull-down menu to change from keyword to publication title.

Even though I discovered that General OneFile indexes thirteen Arizona publications, I will not get a lot of results from the search shown in figure 5.6 because the biggest newspapers in the state, the *Arizona Republic* in Phoenix and the *Arizona Daily Star* in Tucson, are not included in this particular database. In fact, they are indexed in two different, competing databases. The *Arizona Republic* is in ProQuest Newsstand. The *Daily Star* is in Newsbank Access World News, which indexes lots of regional and local newspapers, such as the *Pinal Nugget* and the *Surprise Independent* (nope, not making those up). Figure 5.6 shows the beginning of the list of eighty Arizona news sources indexed in Newsbank's Access World News.

The greatest likelihood of your getting free access to Access World News is through a college or university library. Since many local newspapers

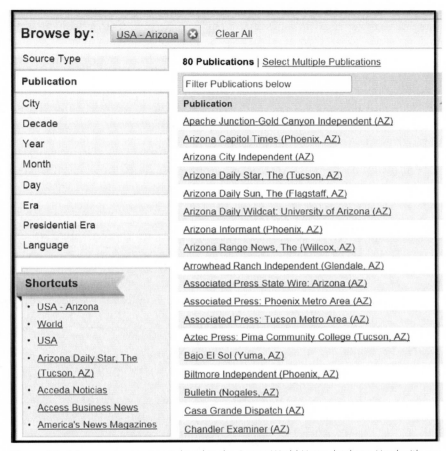

Figure 5.6. Arizona news sources indexed in the Access World News database. Used with permission of Newsbank, Inc.

make their contents searchable on the web and charge small fees for full articles, you may prefer to go that route rather than travel to a library to use Access World News. For some quite small newspapers, there may be only a small web presence, so your only hope for finding full articles may be a commercial database at your local academic library. Let's take a look at Access World News to see how potentially powerful it is for researching prospective donors.

Pretty much everybody in Arizona knows the name Jim Click, owner of major car dealerships and a reputation for generosity. We'll search for stories about him and his giving. Newspaper reporters are trained to put the most important information in the first paragraph or two of any news story. Those first sentences are called the "lead," and the Newsbank search system lets you limit your keywords to the headline and lead. If we do that, we'll avoid retrieving articles that mention Mr. Click at the end of a story that's mostly about someone else entirely. We'll input his name in quotation marks so the system searches it as a phrase. With a name like Click, a common word denoting a sound, it's best to use the quotation marks, because they tell the system to search those words in that order with only a space in between the first and last names.

As a successful big-time business owner, he's in the news a lot for all kinds of things. So let's limit our results to the stories in which his charitable gifts are the focus, as shown in figure 5.7. And, since charitable gifts are sometimes called donations and sometimes contributions, we'll use the term *or* to tell the search system that his name with any one of those three words will be of interest to us.

Notice that we haven't limited by publication title. We can, using the pull-down menu to the left of the search box to select **Source,** which is what Access World News calls the publications it indexes. First thing, we browsed by publication to reassure ourselves that many local Arizona newspapers, periodicals, and even broadcasts are indexed in this database, and since Mr. Click is more of a regional than a national figure, most if not all of

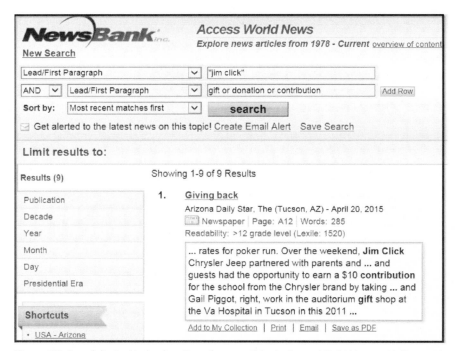

Figure 5.7. Search limited to lead section of news articles in Access World News, with first result. Used with permission of Newsbank, Inc.

our results will likely come from Arizona sources. Since we're interested in learning more about the kinds of causes Mr. Click supports, we don't want to limit our search too much as we begin our research.

The nine results, all from local publications, introduce us to a philanthropist who has supported animal welfare, public safety, food banks, and college sports facilities. A bit more searching with some different keywords will turn up more causes, no doubt. Now we are getting a sense of what our prospect values, and we can decide if his interests match our organization's needs. If so, then we can do further research to find stories about his business and how much it and he might be worth. (Okay, now I sound crass, but let's face it, that's what prospecting for donors is about: not just the potential donor's interests but how large a contribution it might be reasonable to request.)

If the company that made the prospect rich is publicly traded, you can use the SEC's EDGAR database (as we did in chapter 3) to find quarterly and annual reports providing full disclosure of the company's finances and proxy statements documenting the compensation of board members and executives. It's much harder to find such information for private companies, so searching newspaper and magazine indexes by company name may be your best bet for those.

You can try the database Biography in Context, which may be available for free on the web via your state library or your local public or academic library. You can browse the home page categories to find "Native Americans" or "Religious Leaders." But for our philanthropic purposes, use the search box in the upper right to input a prospective donor's name. With more than 700,000 biographical entries, the database may still fall short when it comes to your local heroes. But if you are aiming big, it might be quite helpful.

Let's give it a try.

The best way to search is last name first. In fact, stop at the last name and see what your options are, as shown in figure 5.8.

Biography in Context gives us some helpful data so we can decide which Buffet we want to know more about. In this case, it's Howard G., the philanthropist. Clicking on his name takes you to the biographical entries in two different sources included in the database.

Because Buffet has written a number of books, he has a write-up in *Contemporary Authors Online*, a biographical dictionary of published authors. And he has a biographical sketch within Biography in Context. Clicking on each of the two references will take you to the full text of each biographical sketch. The two entries state that his philanthropy focuses on fighting hunger worldwide. So if you're prospecting for funds to build a state-of-the-art cat shelter, you may want to keep looking.

We've used Biography in Context to discover information about people who might want to give to our charitable organization. The database can

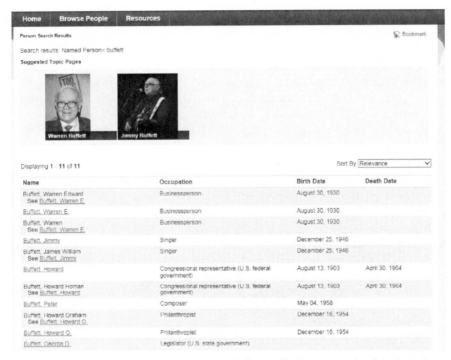

Figure 5.8. List of the people with the last name Buffett profiled in a biographical database. From Biography in Context. © Gale, a part of Cengage Learning, Inc. Reproduced by permission www.cengage.com/permissions.

be used any time you need to find information about individuals, such as a world leader you are writing a paper about, a person whose books you love to read, or a famous musician who inspires you.

WHY IT WORKS

We used freely available websites focused exclusively on charities to find information about nonprofit organizations.

To find local information, we identified and used databases that index local and regional periodicals and news outlets.

In addition to searching by organizations' names, we searched for people's names to find sources of funding for specific needs.

Good point: Conducting searches using a well-selected variety of websites, news indexes, and biographical resources can yield powerful information presented from different perspectives.

NOTE

1. "Giving USA: Americans Gave $335.17 Billion to Charity in 2013; Total Approaches Pre-Recession Peak," http://www.philanthropy.iupui.edu/news/article/giving-usa-2014

CHAPTER 6

Here's to Your Health

Lumps, spots, coughing, fatigue—a lot can go wrong with our bodies and minds! Before you scare yourself by reading health-related horror stories found with a bit of quick web searching, let's deploy some strategies for finding authoritative information. Whether you have recently been diagnosed with a health condition, are trying to avoid such a diagnosis, are helping an ill friend or family member, or are doing research for a course of study, the resources and techniques in this chapter will yield valuable information.

By the time you complete the exercises in this chapter, you will be able to

- easily limit web engine search results to authoritative government sites;
- search and browse for health-related information on the U.S. government's web portal;
- understand when and how to use two major health-sciences resources, MedlinePlus and PubMed; and
- find articles about medical conditions and health issues in a database indexing scientific periodicals.

Let's begin with a condition that involves both body and mind: heroin addiction. I'd like to learn more about the medical aspects. If I Google it, the screen of results list paid ads at the top and to the right for commercial products and services to help people quit the drug, shown in figure 6.1. The first non-paid link is to a residential treatment center and the second link is to a foundation, and both sites offer some information about heroin addiction. The next links, under the Google heading "In the News," are to stories that seem to be mostly about famous names, and then, if we persist in scrolling down, we get back to some regular links including one good

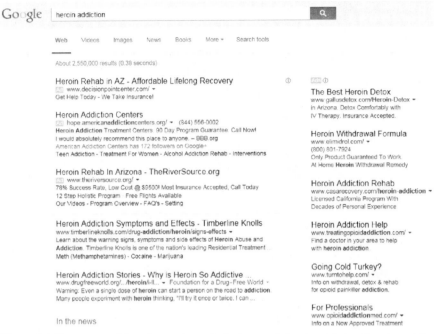

Figure 6.1. First screen of Google search results for keywords *heroin addiction*. Google and the Google logo are registered trademarks of Google Inc., used with permission.

one: www.drugabuse.gov. That's a federal government website that we can count on to have authoritative information.

In fact, the U.S. government spends a lot of money supporting health-related research and gathering, analyzing, and publishing health-related information. One hidden feature you can use with Google, and with the nontracking search engine DuckDuckGo.com, is to limit by site by adding the following limiter right in the same search box with your keywords: *site:gov*. The results will be limited to any dot-gov sites that include federal, state, and local government agencies.

In many cases, it's best to start a search that's limited to government sites when your health is at stake, and one of the easiest ways to do that is to start at the U.S. government's main information portal, USA.gov. As you can see in figure 6.2, the top of the USA.gov home page offers a navigation bar with links you can click on to browse for government agencies, elected officials, health information, housing information, and so forth. Browsing links works well when you don't know much about a topic and when you are a new visitor to an information-heavy website. After a while, drilling down link by link can get tedious. That's why USA.gov offers a search box on the home page, for those of us in a hurry.

Figure 6.2. Navigation bar and search box at the top of the USA.gov home page.

If we input *heroin addiction* in the search box, we receive links to information from a variety of federal and state government agencies (see figure 6.3). Of course, the by-now-familiar DRUGABUSE.gov site appears multiple times for its different web pages of information on the drug heroin, drug addictions, and heroin addiction. By skimming the URLs, we can see that the National Institutes of Health (nih.gov), the Centers for Disease Control (cdc.gov), and even New York State's Health Department (health.ny.gov) offer information related to heroin addiction.

First, there are no paid ads to try to ignore. Second, you don't have to scroll to find the worthwhile links. And www.drugabuse.gov appears in the

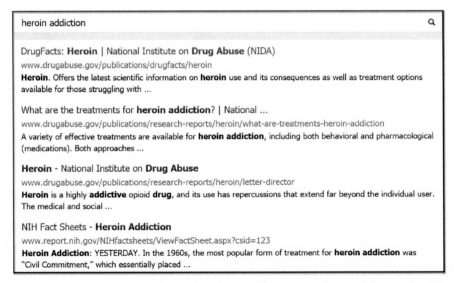

Figure 6.3. The top results when searching *heroin addiction* using the search box on the USA .gov home page.

first three results, followed by a link to information at the NIH (the National Institutes of Health), then three more results from www.drugabuse .gov, followed by a link for a service called MedlinePlus from the National Library of Medicine. None of these links tries to sell you any products or services or memberships, and none asks for a donation (because, well, you already gave, if you're an American taxpayer).

The National Library of Medicine and the National Institutes of Health make a gigantic database of information available for free on the web, PubMed. With more than twenty-four million records to articles about health, including links to a lot of complete articles, PubMed can be kind of overwhelming. Most of the articles are written by and for professionals working in the biomedical and health sciences fields, so there's a ton of technical jargon and mathematical formulas in the articles. PubMed uses Medical Subject Headings (MeSH), a thesaurus of preferred terms to help us find what we need in those twenty-four million items in the database. But first, think carefully about why you might want to use PubMed at all.

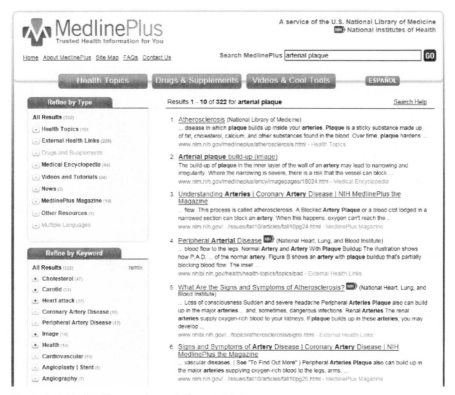

Figure 6.4. MedlinePlus search results for *arterial plaque*.

As we saw with the USA.gov portal, there's a service called MedlinePlus that's designed for laypersons, those of us who don't know or care about arterial plaque until our doctors tell us we have too darn much of it for our own good. If we want to learn about arterial plaque, we can use USA.gov, or we can go straight to MedlinePlus, http://www.nlm.nih.gov/medlineplus/, put our keywords *arterial plaque* in the search box, and find accurate, up-to-date information based on scientific research, as figure 6.4 shows.

For that particular search, the first result is one of the best. One thing we learn is that the medical term for plaque-clogged arteries is the almost unpronounceable *atherosclerosis*. If we want to do more digging, knowing that term will be key to finding good information. MedlinePlus uses medical terms like that, but it presents information in clear language and includes illustrations that help us understand. If we do the same search in the box on the PubMed.gov page, we get different results (see figure 6.5).

Not only do we get far too many results, but they are about all kinds of things regarding atherosclerosis: macrophages, oxidized cardiolipin, gold nonparticles. We need to narrow our search. For this exercise, we're interested in treating atherosclerosis by changing our diet. We're going to use the search form to help us, so click on the little **Advanced** link under the search box on the home page.

In addition to using two additional search terms—treatment and diet—we're going to use the pull-down menu to the left of the search boxes to

Figure 6.5. First results from keyword search for *atherosclerosis* in the PubMed database.

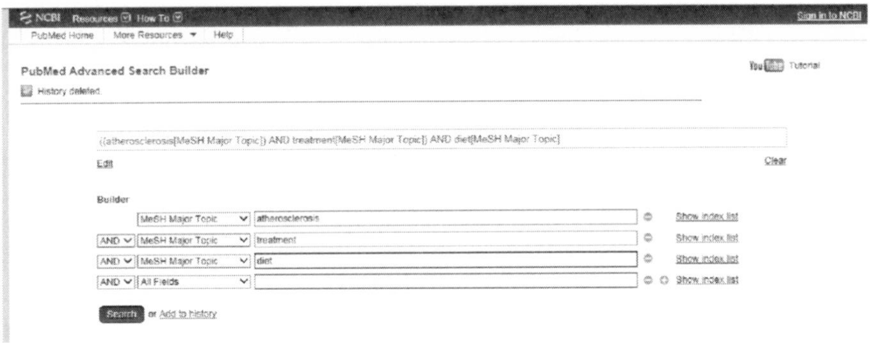

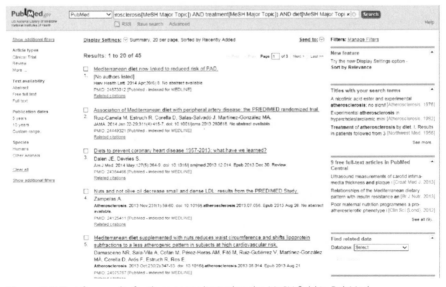

Figure 6.6. Use of the PubMed advanced search form to limit query terms to the MeSH Field.

limit our search to MeSH topics (see figure 6.6). We are telling the search system not to look for our three terms anywhere they happen to appear, but to look for them only when they appear as MeSH terms connected to the article. In other words, someone has looked at the article and decided if it is focused on atherosclerosis, rather than casually mentioning the condition. If the indexer decides it's about atherosclerosis, he or she tags it with the MeSH term *atherosclerosis* in the database record, where you'll also see the names of the authors, the title of the article, which journal the article was published in, and in which issue and where (indicated by the page numbers) in the issue the article appears. If the article is also about treatment, it gets tagged with the MeSH term *treatment*, and if it includes a substantive

Figure 6.7. First few results for three terms limited to the MeSH field in PubMed.

discussion about diet, it gets tagged with the MeSH term *diet*. Each of the search boxes is separated by the word *and*, which tells the system to find and bring back only the items that have been tagged with all three MeSH terms. This technique retrieves forty-five results, as figure 6.7 shows, and they are all relevant to our question. But that doesn't mean they are any more readable by the likes of us. Your best bet if you use PubMed is to take the results to your physician to open a discussion on the health condition and the possible treatment options.

So far we've been using openly and freely available web resources, and they have worked well. But let's look at one last resource, a commercial database, before we close this chapter. From Gale, a major database provider, Science in Context is designed to help students of all ages learn. This is an

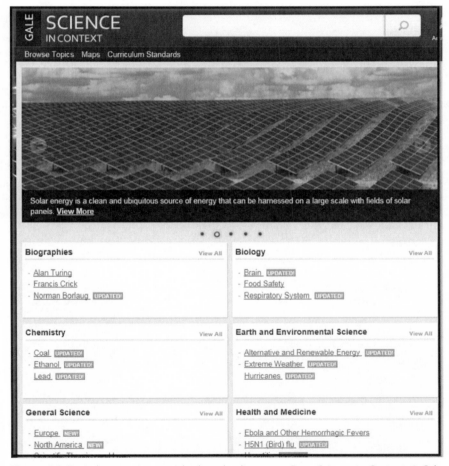

Figure 6.8. Topical categories on a database landing page. From Science in Context. © Gale, a part of Cengage Learning, Inc. Reproduced by permission www.cengage.com/permissions.

advantage for health information because it means that most of what we find will be understandable. The disadvantage is that it's a commercial database, so its services don't come free. But if you're lucky, your state, public, or academic library pays for you to have free access.

The home page of Science in Context organizes information into broad categories, including Health and Medicine (see figure 6.8). Under that heading are links to information about three hot topics, whatever has been in the news lately.

You can click on the tiny **View All** link to see other topics. You can find health topics in the alphabetical links and keep drilling down to the topic that interests you. For instance, you can click on a mental health topic such

Figure 6.9. The Science in Context page on depression. From Science in Context. © Gale, a part of Cengage Learning, Inc. Reproduced by permission www.cengage.com/permissions.

as depression to be taken to a page offering an overview of the topic plus links to reference tools such as encyclopedias, news stories, and research articles, as figure 6.9 shows.

And, as we've come to expect by now, you can skip all the navigating and instead use the search box on the home page. If you input *depression*, the result will be the same main page you arrived at by drilling down through the links.

To limit your search to journal articles, use the tiny **More** pull-down menu above the search box to make that selection. With more than two thousand results, as shown in figure 6.10, we know there are ways to focus in on the topic. One easy way, as always, is to add search terms for other aspects of the condition, such as therapy or prescription drugs. The left-side column offers easy ways to limit: by subject, document types, and title of the periodical in which the article was published. If we recognize the journal *Science* by its name and reputation as an authoritative publication,

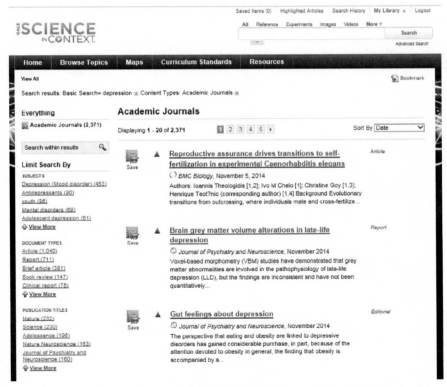

Figure 6.10. First results from a search for the topic *depression* limited to articles in academic journals, with additional filters on the left. From Science in Context. © Gale, a part of Cengage Learning, Inc. Reproduced by permission www.cengage.com/permissions.

we can click on that link and see 230 records to articles on depression that *Science* has published. Once we have a list of the 230 articles, clicking on the title of each one will show the complete text of the article.

Health is one of the most popular topics people research. The resources and methods covered in this chapter offer some efficient ways to get through the mass of health information, even as more is produced every day.

WHY IT WORKS

We used freely available federal government databases on the web, one for health consumers and one for health professionals, to find authoritative information.

We also used a commercial database dedicated to the topic of science to find health information.

Our strategies included browsing through categories and subcategories to learn more about our topic as we drilled down, as well as using traditional keyword searching.

Good point: Using a website or database focused on the subject area you are researching automatically eliminates a lot of irrelevant information, such as searching science databases for clinical depression and searching history databases for economic depression.

PART II

How and Why It Works

CHAPTER 7

Make It Work for You

The first six chapters introduced you to some of the major commercial and open-access databases available for finding the information you need, along with exercises and examples to get you right into searching them. The next five chapters detail some of the more technical aspects of databases and the methods for retrieving relevant information from them. This chapter revisits the databases to reinforce key points and discusses some creative ways to use databases to your advantage. If you understand how and why database searching works, you can make it work for you.

Among the commercial databases introduced in the first chapters were

- General OneFile, Academic OneFile, Biography in Context, and Science in Context, all on the Gale Cengage platform;
- MasterFILE Premier and Academic Search Complete, on the EBSCO-host platform;
- Statistical Insight and ABI/Inform, from ProQuest; and
- Access World News, from Newsbank.

Among the openly available federal government resources covered were

- the SEC's EDGAR database of publicly traded companies' financial reports;
- the Census Bureau's American FactFinder, for data related to population and the economy;
- the IRS's directory of nonprofit organizations;
- the main federal government portal, USA.gov; and
- specialized federal government services such as Grants.gov and MedlinePlus.

Multipurpose databases such as General and Academic OneFile, MasterFILE Premier, and Academic Search Complete are designed to help you find information on whatever you're researching. They're broad and big, increasing your chances of finding at least an article or two no matter how obscure the topic. They have the added advantage of indexing articles going back a few decades, plus they deliver full text of many of the more recent articles, saving you from having to track articles down in a physical library or pay for digital copies on the publisher's website.

FROM GENERAL TO SPECIFIC

While such multipurpose databases present great places to start a search, they aren't always where you should end a search. You're bound to find something useful on a topic you're researching for a college-level course or for a work-related project. Be aware that there are scholarly databases that run deep rather than broad, indexing information in one subject area or scholarly discipline. As we saw with the business index ABI/Inform, a subject-specific database enables deep research that includes articles on business and industry in general-interest periodicals and in business journals as well as special reports published outside the customary periodicals.

Another example is the American Psychological Association's database, PsycINFO, currently with more than three million records, each record representing research articles and other scholarly material. The database indexes peer-reviewed behavioral sciences journals, and anyone looking for information related to mental health should consider PsycINFO first. Another example is a database created and maintained by the American Economic Association, EconLit, which includes more than one million records for material going back to the late nineteenth century, indexing articles as well as dissertations, books, and working papers.

Sometimes it's best to use one of these more focused databases rather than, or in addition to, the broad scholarly databases like Academic One-

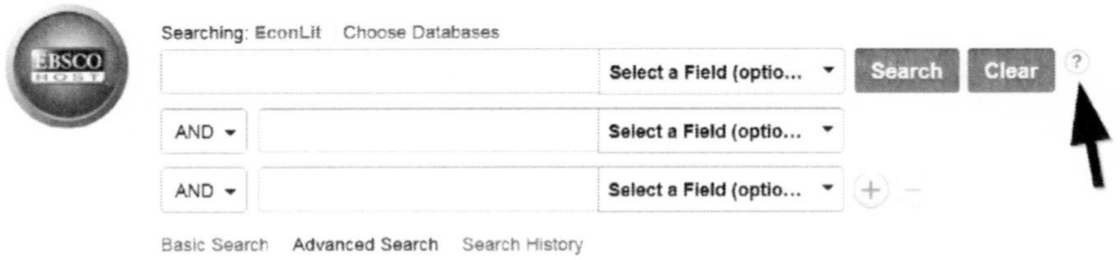

Figure 7.1. EBSCOHost advanced search screen for the EconLit database. The arrow is pointing to the question mark icon for accessing the help system. © 2015 EBSCO Industries, Inc. Used with permission of EBSCO Information Services.

File and Academic Search Complete. Each database has its own special features and strengths, of course, but if you're familiar with the platform it's on, you'll have a head start with searching effectively. If you have used EBSCOhost's Academic Search Complete, you'll be comforted by the familiar look and feel of EBSCOhost's offering of PsycINFO and EconLit. For instance, the EBSCO search screen always offers a small question mark icon in the upper right, shown in figure 7.1, where you can find help no matter which database you're searching on the EBSCO platform.

One oddity about help on EBSCO is that it always presents generic instructions and tips that work with any database on the platform. If you want help specific to the database you're in, you'll need to scroll all the way to the end of the menu in the left-hand column of the help screen to find it (see figure 7.2).

I don't know why EBSCO puts database-specific help there, but at least it's consistent and you can always find it there. An example of information and help specific to the EconLit database indexing economic publications is shown in figure 7.3.

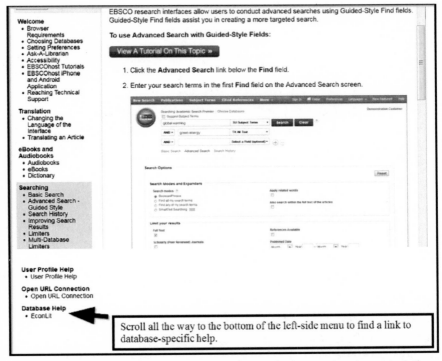

Figure 7.2. EBSCO help screens explain search tips for any database on the company's platform. Database-specific help is the last link on the menu. From EconLit. © 2015 EBSCO Industries, Inc. Used with permission of EBSCO Information Services.

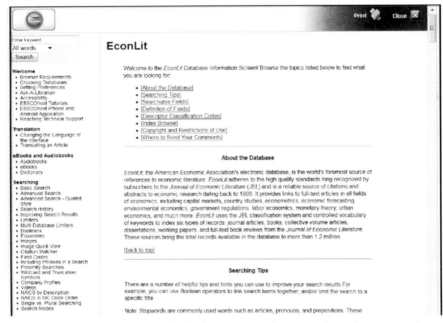

Figure 7.3. Help screen for a specific database, giving information about the topics and time period covered, searchable fields, and special features unique to this database. From EconLit. © 2015 EBSCO Industries, Inc. Used with permission of EBSCO Information Services.

You can visit the websites of the various vendors such as Gale Cengage, EBSCO, ProQuest, and Newsbank to discover what databases exist and then check with your library to see if it subscribes to the ones you want to use.

A bit more about platforms: each database vendor serves up its menu of databases on a different platform. The term "platform" can mean different things, but what I mean here is the combination of interface and system that makes it possible for you to search a database. The interface is made up of the screens that sit between you and the database, including the design of the search boxes, the little lines of instructions or examples offered near the search boxes, and the way results are presented after you do a search. The system includes the searchable records representing articles, book chapters, and other forms of information as well as the indexing of the words in those records so they are findable and retrievable, and the software that makes the search engine work the way it does. The American Psychological Association sells access to its databases right on its website on a platform it calls PsycNET. But the association has contracts with commercial database vendors EBSCO and ProQuest, so your library may offer it on the EBSCO or ProQuest platform. Libraries often buy access to bundles of databases from a single vendor, so if your library has Academic Search Complete from

EBSCO, chances are good it will provide access to PsycINFO and other specialized databases via EBSCO as well.

Now that you know there are hundreds of databases indexing scholarly information, you might want to visit your library's website to see which ones are available to you. Library websites usually offer a link to a list of the databases they offer access to, so look around a bit to find it. You may find a link to an alphabetical list of databases as well as links by subject areas. You might be surprised by the number of research databases your local academic, public, and state libraries make available to you.

Commercial vendors of databases want customers, and one way to keep customers using their products is by having customers know about and understand those products. That's one reason they include the little question mark icons that lead to help screens and tutorials. The more you learn about a database, what it indexes, and how it can be searched, the more likely you are to go back and use it again, with confidence it will yield the treasures you seek. As we have seen, databases tell you which publications they index and how far back their indexing goes. If a database doesn't index the journal you're looking for or the newspaper in your city when you need local news, no need to waste your time searching it. It's not hard to check database by database for the publications indexed as you are deciding which database to search for information related to your research project. Your library might make it easier still, by providing a list of e-journals—periodicals in electronic form—and where each one is indexed.

While you're poking around a library's website scoping out the databases, you might look for a list of e-journals. Some e-journals charge libraries subscription fees, and some are open-access journals, meaning they are freely available on the web. Some libraries will include notes under each e-journal title indicating which database indexes the journal and the time period included. Some libraries make the e-journal's title a link. If you click on a title link, you may be prompted to search the contents of that journal or you may be given a list of all the available issues. You can browse issue by issue; that's a great way to get to know a journal and to get to know the subject area or academic discipline that is the focus of the journal. Browsing like that is definitely something I recommend for a graduate student or a new professional. For an undergraduate student, though, it might be a bit of a time sink if you are looking for articles on a specific topic.

For most research questions, it's better to search a database that indexes lots of different journals. An exception might be an undergraduate who knows about a journal covering his or her field wanting to get to know the field better. For example, a plant sciences major might want to skim issues of a research journal called *Botany*, one of several science-related journals published by NRC Research Press. A journalism student might want to browse each issue of the highly respected *Columbia Journalism Review*. To be clear, *CJR* falls into another category of journal. It is a trade journal, devoted to publishing articles about journalists, journalism, and the media business. For people in personnel management, an important trade journal is *HR Professionals Magazine*. Large databases such as Academic Search Complete will index popular and trade magazines and scholarly journals. All three kinds of articles may show up in your search results, along with newspaper articles, book chapters, and dissertations, depending on the database. If you are writing a term paper requiring you to cite scholarly research, you will want to look at your results carefully to make sure you are not choosing a popular or trade magazine article to download and use. And you may want to use the database search engine's filters to eliminate popular articles if you only want research articles.

Searching different databases on the same platform helps reinforce your skill with the particular functions and features of the vendor's search system. Searching different databases on different platforms may slow you down a bit at first as you get accustomed to the new look and feel of the interface and the way the search engine operates. Nevertheless, there are only so many different ways to organize information and make it retrievable. All commercial bibliographic databases will let you search for known items—books or articles or dissertations or reports, depending on what the database indexes—that you know exist and whose title or author you know. Okay, maybe not the whole title, but just a couple of keywords, and maybe the author's last name because your professor was talking too fast when she suggested you read it for your term paper. Anyway, if you are looking for a known item, you understand from the searches covered in the first section of this book that you can use pull-down menus to limit your search to the keywords in a title or to the names in the author field. It doesn't matter what the interface looks like, there's bound to be a way to limit to authors and/or titles, even both at the same time; knowing that, you might want to look carefully at any new (to you) search screen to familiarize yourself quickly with the options it offers.

When you aren't looking for known items, when you're looking for items you hope exist because they would answer your questions and help you accomplish your goals, you can use whatever terms you can fathom for your topic and plug them into the default search boxes on whatever database search screen is in front of you. But you know you can discover the preferred terms for your topic—by looking them up in the thesaurus within the database or by doing a quick search and then identifying the subject terms attached to the best results—and then use those preferred terms to get the best results quickly. One thing you may have noticed is that competing vendors or different databases might label preferred terms in different ways. In one database they might be called "subject headings," such as in PubMed, which uses Medical Subject Headings labeled MeSH. In another, they might be called "subjects," while another might call them "descriptors." As long as you understand they are the controlled-vocabulary terms the experts have blessed as the best for each topic and that if you use them you won't have to guess all the possible natural-language terms for the same topic, you're golden.

Oh, but wait: a cautionary note about controlled vocabulary, whether it takes the form of subject headings, descriptors, or subjects. If you are researching a new phenomenon or issue, it's possible the experts haven't gotten around to meeting, debating, and settling on the preferred term for it yet. So you might have to use a broader controlled vocabulary term that does already exist, in which case you may retrieve information that's a little too broad for your new topic. Another alternative is to use the natural-language terms you've seen used in news stories or other sources discussing your topic, and use the Boolean *or* to include a few synonyms or variant spellings.

Perhaps this is the perfect moment to mention that successful information searching is an art as well as a science.

GETTING CREATIVE

When you find new uses for a familiar database, you're getting creative with your research skills. In chapter 4, for instance, we used the Census Bureau's data service, American FactFinder, to find population counts and characteristics. Nothing's stopping you from wandering over to the main web page of the Census Bureau (census.gov) to find reports, such as *Remarriage in the United States*; infographics, such as a color-coded map of manufacturing activity in the United States; and a list of online tutorials to help you make full use of the agency's data. In chapter 6, we used Science in Context to find health information, but the database can be used to find material on a variety of topics useful to the student designing a science-fair project, writing a paper on the environmental aspects of coal-fired power plants, or researching the life of a prominent zoologist.

In chapter 5, when we were researching philanthropists to learn about the kinds of causes they contributed to, we discovered that General OneFile indexes some local newspapers and magazines and Fodor's travel guides. Your local public library probably owns a lot of the Fodor's travel guides, and if your library is like the one where I live, most of them are checked out to other people most of the time. Nice to know that General OneFile offers an alternative, where you can find travel information on the city, state, or country you are planning to visit and download it or print it. For vacation daydreaming, try doing a publication search for *fodor's* to see a list of the more than three hundred travel guides indexed in General OneFile, as shown in figure 7.4.

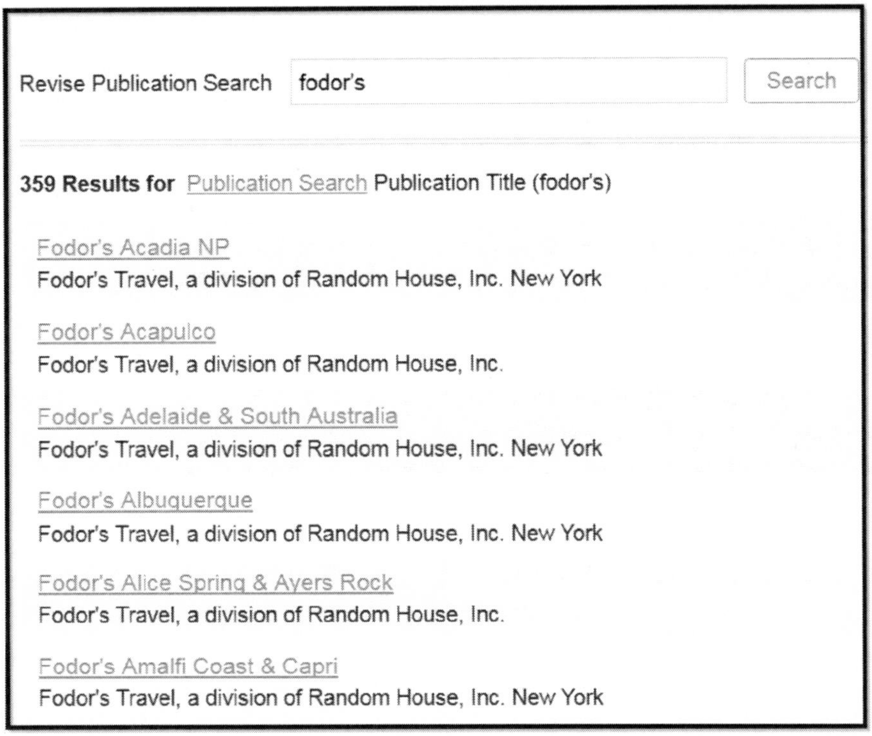

| Revise Publication Search | fodor's | Search |

---

359 Results for Publication Search Publication Title (fodor's)

Fodor's Acadia NP
Fodor's Travel, a division of Random House, Inc. New York

Fodor's Acapulco
Fodor's Travel, a division of Random House, Inc.

Fodor's Adelaide & South Australia
Fodor's Travel, a division of Random House, Inc. New York

Fodor's Albuquerque
Fodor's Travel, a division of Random House, Inc. New York

Fodor's Alice Spring & Ayers Rock
Fodor's Travel, a division of Random House, Inc.

Fodor's Amalfi Coast & Capri
Fodor's Travel, a division of Random House, Inc. New York

Figure 7.4. Beginning of the alphabetical list of travel guides published by Fodor's indexed in the database. From General OneFile. © Gale, a part of Cengage Learning, Inc. Reproduced by permission www.cengage.com/permissions.

When you are searching General OneFile, you can use the advanced search form to input a place-name in one search box and then in the next search box input *fodor's* and change from a **Keyword** to a **Publication Title** search. Of course, if you don't limit to Fodor's travel guides, you may retrieve them along with other travel stories published in any of the periodicals indexed by General OneFile when you input a place-name and a keyword such as *travel* or *vacation*.

Limiting to the **Publication Title** field offers a bit more flexibility than it might seem to at first glance. If you want to limit your results to a single periodical title, for instance, you can do so by inputting the title in the search box and using the pull-down menu to select **Publication Title**. But you don't have to input a complete and exact title; the Gale search system is programmed to look for keywords wherever they appear in the **Publication Title** field. If you are seeking reviews and recommendations regarding a consumer product you are planning to purchase, you can input a keyword for the product in one search box and then input the word *consumer* in the next search box and limit it to **Publication Title**. All the results will be from indexed periodicals and reference books that have the word *consumer* in their titles, such as *Consumer Guide Magazine* and *Consumer Reports Annual Buying Guide*.

Keep an open mind about openly accessible resources, such as those available from the federal government. If you are researching consumer products, you might remember hearing about a product recall that the federal government required a company to issue. That could spark a search on USA.gov for product recalls and for other kinds of consumer information, including scam alerts, identity theft protection tips, and similar topics. As you know, the federal government has an agency for almost everything, and most of them collect and disseminate information of one kind or another. The best information seekers—and finders—do not limit their searches to commercial databases. They broaden their searching to include open resources such as those provided by

- federal, state, and local government agencies and the military, on .gov, .mil, and .us sites;
- colleges and universities, on .edu sites;
- publicly traded businesses, especially full disclosure of financial data for investors, at .com sites; and
- nongovernmental and nonprofit organizations, at .org sites.

The more you know about effective information searching, the more you can make it work for you. The remainder of this book helps you achieve another level of search expertise.

CHAPTER 8

The Elements of Search

The search process involves four key elements:

- Database
- Search system
- Interface
- Searcher (you)

The database contains information, the search system makes it possible to retrieve the information, the interface serves as the representative of the database and its search system, and you use your knowledge of the database and your search skills to find the information you need. We'll address each element in order.

THE DATABASE

A database is a collection of records. Each record contains data that uniquely identify an information item such as a book, a newspaper story, or a magazine article. One record = one information item. Records are structured so the different aspects used to describe an information item are presented in a consistent and predictable way (see figure 8.1). A record is structured into fields, and each field has a designated purpose. For example, the author's last name will be in a field of the record designated to contain only authors' last names. Depending on the decisions the database creator has made, the field might be for the whole name of the author. And there's probably another field for the second author and for the third one, if the item was written by more than one person. The record may have a field for the main title of the book or article and another field for the subtitle. Other fields will contain

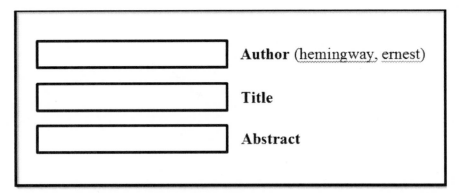

Figure 8.1. A database record structures different elements of a publication into their corresponding fields, which are then indexed so they can be searched. The text to the right of the author box indicates how author names should be input and how they should be searched in the database.

further identifying information, such as publisher or journal name, volume number, issue number, page numbers, and date. Some databases have records representing technical reports, government documents (such as congressional hearings), conference proceedings, and other items that are not journal articles. Sometimes a "document type" field will indicate whether the item is an article, conference proceeding, hearing, book review, dissertation, or even book, among other possibilities. The record may include an abstract summarizing the article, which would be input in the abstract field, and it may include a link to the full text or full image of the article. The record may even include the entire text of the article in a big full-text field.

SEARCH SYSTEM

When you search a database, you aren't actually searching the records themselves. The search system—sometimes called the search engine or the retrieval system—does a lot of work behind the scenes. It actually searches indexes that are generated from the structured information in the records. It's an efficient and effective method for quickly retrieving the records that match your search query.

To create the author index, the indexing program runs through all the records and grabs all the authors' names from the author and coauthor fields and throws them in a big file. Each name in the author index file is linked to every record where that name appears. Similarly, for the abstract index, the indexing program grabs every substantive word (not common little words like *the*) and throws them in a file, with a link from each word to each record where it appears in the abstract. Indexing is what makes names and words searchable and records retrievable.

A field may be keyword indexed or phrase indexed or both. About the only time it matters is in author name searching. In keyword indexing, every substantive keyword is searchable; it becomes what information professionals call an access point, meaning the keyword gives you access to the record where it appears. Of course, the retrieval system doesn't know what a word means; it is programmed to index any string of characters from the alphabet that occur between two spaces. For a computer, that's the definition of a word.

With phrase indexing, the system indexes every character including the spaces in a phrase. If the author field is keyword indexed, you can input *joe smith* (most retrieval systems are programmed to ignore capital letters) and get all the records that have the word *joe* in any of the author fields and all of the records that have the word *smith* in any of the author fields. In contrast, if the author field is only phrase indexed, and authors' names are listed last name first in the index file, then you must input the author's name last name first to get results. In our example, you'd have to input *smith, joe* to retrieve all the records in which he's listed as the author. If you ever do an author search in a database and get zero results, it could be that you input first name first when the system only understands last name first.

Sometimes records will have a field that's not indexed and thus not searchable, but it may still be useful to you when you see it in a set of results because it may tell you something extra about an item that's good to know. For example, a record representing a magazine article will include the page numbers, so you'll know where to look in the magazine for that article, but page numbers themselves may not be indexed and so aren't searchable. No great loss, though, since people are more likely to search by author name and/or title keywords or topics than by page numbers. If you know the page numbers of an article, you probably don't need to search a database to find the article, right?

The great thing about indexed fields, in addition to making it possible to retrieve results, is that they offer you some sophisticated ways to retrieve only the results you want. That's where understanding the search interface becomes important.

INTERFACE

The search interface sits between you and the database. It is the public face of the search system. The search screen that opens up when you log in to a database is a major part of the interface. It offers obvious search boxes, and intuitively you know to input keywords in the boxes to get results. But the

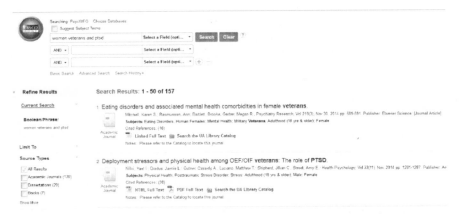

Figure 8.2. Brief records screen showing the first two results of a search for *women veterans and ptsd*. From PsycINFO. © 2015 EBSCO Industries, Inc. Used with permission of EBSCO Information Services.

interface offers more than what's on the search screen at first glance, usually in the form of pull-down menus next to the search boxes that let you limit your searches to particular fields—or more accurately, indexes—of the records. Depending on how the fields of the records are indexed, it may be possible to search by author name, by title or title keywords, by substantive keywords in the abstract, or any number of other ways.

Once you've input keywords and used the pull-down menus and then activated your search, the interface may take the form of two kinds of results screens. The first displays a list of brief records for you to browse and choose from (see figure 8.2).

The second kind of results screen displays the full record, giving you more information about the item you selected from the list of brief records (see figure 8.3).

Figure 8.3 shows the record representing an article titled "Eating Disorders and Associated Mental Health Comorbidities in Female Veterans," which has four authors and was published in a scholarly journal called *Psychiatry Research*. The full record for this article gives you enough information to decide whether you want to read the whole article.

When you are at a search screen or a results screen, it's wise to take a moment to read everything on it. You likely will see little prompts and tips to help you get started. Often the upper right of the screen features a small "help" link that you can use to read more in-depth information about the search system's capabilities and the database's contents. If you scroll down a search screen, you may discover ways to limit your search, for instance, to a particular time period. And on a results screen, looking to the left may yield a menu of options for understanding how the results break down into

Eating disorders and associated mental health comorbidities in female **veterans**.

Authors: Mitchell, Karen S., **Women's** Health Sciences Division, National Center for PTSD, VA Boston Healthcare System, Boston, MA, US, ksmitche@bu.edu
Rasmusson, Ann, **Women's** Health Sciences Division, National Center for PTSD, VA Boston Healthcare System, Boston, MA, US
Bartlett, Brooke, **Women's** Health Sciences Division, National Center for PTSD, VA Boston Healthcare System, Boston, MA, US
Gerber, Megan R., VA Boston Healthcare System, Boston, MA, US

Address: Mitchell, Karen S., WHSD, National Center for PTSD, VA Boston Healthcare System, (116B-3), 150 South Huntington Avenue, Boston, MA, US, 02130, ksmitche@bu.edu

Source: Psychiatry Research, Vol 219(3), Nov 30, 2014. pp. 589-591.

Page Count: 3

Publisher: Netherlands : Elsevier Science

ISSN: 0165-1781 (Print)

Language: English

Keywords: disordered eating, **women**, mental health

Abstract: Eating disorders (EDs) remain understudied among **veterans**, possibly due to the perception that primarily male population does not suffer from EDs. However, previous research suggests that male and female **veterans** do experience EDs. The high rates of posttraumatic stress disorder (PTSD), depression, and obesity observed among **veterans** may make this group vulnerable to disordered eating. Retrospective chart review was used to examine data from 492 female **veterans** who were presented to a **women's** primary care center at a large, urban VA medical center between 2007 and 2009. A total of 2.8% of this sample had been diagnosed with an ED. In bivariate analyses, presence of **PTSD** and depression were significantly associated with having an ED diagnosis. However, when these two disorders were included in a multivariate model controlling for age, only depression diagnosis and lower age were significantly related to ED status. In sum, the rate of EDs in this sample is comparable to prevalence estimates of EDs in the general population. Current findings underscore the importance of assessing for EDs among VA patients and the need for further research among **veterans**. (PsycINFO Database Record (c) 2014 APA, all rights reserved) (journal abstract)

Subjects: *Eating Disorders; *Human Females; *Mental Health; *Military Veterans; Comorbidity; Major Depression; Posttraumatic Stress Disorder

PsycINFO Classification: Eating Disorders (3260)
Military Psychology (3800)

Population: Human
Female

Age Group: Adulthood (18 yrs & older)

Methodology: Empirical Study; Quantitative Study

Format Covered: Electronic

Publication Type: Journal; Peer Reviewed Journal

Figure 8.3. Screen showing the full record of the item selected from the brief records screen for the *women veterans and ptsd* search. From PsycINFO. © 2015 EBSCO Industries, Inc. Used with permission of EBSCO Information Services.

different topics or types of material, such as how many are scholarly articles and how many are book reviews.

The Google search screen has trained us all to go fast and not to question if there might be better ways to find what we need. So you may have to force yourself to slow down a bit when you first see a new-to-you search screen. Let it teach you a thing or two about becoming a smarter searcher.

YOU

First, think carefully about the questions you are trying to answer when you approach a database. Is part of the question background information to give you a bit of context? Are you seeking a known item, about which you know the author's name or title or a few keywords from the title, or are you seeking information on a subject? How many different facets does the question have? Is there one topic? Are there subtopics or related topics? Are there aspects of the topic, such as geographic or time-period limitations, that serve to limit or refine the topic? Is there a specific format that is needed?

Second, familiarize yourself with the database before searching it. Learn the kinds of material it indexes, the time period it covers, and the subjects it includes. In many commercial databases, detailed information about database content can be found on the help pages linked from the search screen.

Third, any time you approach a new database, it pays to take some time to scrutinize the search screen. Read any instructions, check out the pull-down

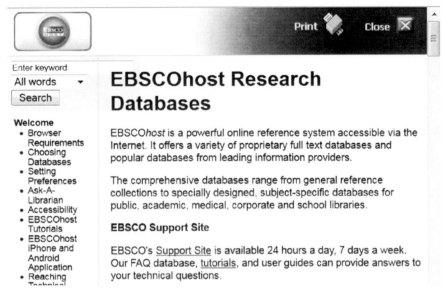

Figure 8.4. Beginning of the EBSCOhost help pages, accessed from the tiny "help" link in the upper right of the database search screen. The search box on the left lets you search the help pages by keywords. © 2015 EBSCO Industries, Inc. Used with permission of EBSCO Information Services.

menus to see what your options are, and scroll down the screen to see if there are any special features or options. Click on any (i) or ? icons to learn more about the database's contents, search engine features, and search tips for that particular database (see figure 8.4). Do a quick and easy search so you can see how results are displayed. From the list of brief records, choose a full record and study it carefully to understand all its fields and contents.

Fourth, once you've formulated a search and tried it, analyze your results. Are there too many? Too few? Are they relevant? Reformulate your search and analyze the new results. There may be a single most efficient search strategy to answer your question, but don't expect it to be the first one you try unless you have lots (and lots) of searching experience.

If you know the database well but start to work in an EBSCO setting rather than a ProQuest setting or on some other platform, you'll have to get used to the unfamiliar search screen, help system, and results screens. As long as you understand the four elements involved in online searching (thinking through your question, familiarizing yourself with the database, scrutinizing the search screen, and analyzing the results), you'll know what to look for regarding search engine capabilities and database scope and contents.

CHAPTER 9

A Map of the Information World

The economy runs on information. In fact, the U.S. Economic Census has a separate category, sector 51, for all the information industries. And believe me, sector 51 is not nearly as mysterious as Nevada's Area 51. According to the 2012 Economic Census, 3.2 million individuals were employed in sector 51, whose many information establishments had a total annual payroll of $263 million and total receipts of $1.2 billion. Sector 51 includes movie production and distribution companies, music studios, broadcasting, telecommunications, libraries and archives, and publishing of all varieties.

Within the information industry are database producers and vendors, making billions of records searchable in thousands of databases. Don't believe me? Go to the website of your favorite university library and take a look at the long list of databases it makes available to students. Or, for a smaller list, go to your state library website (see appendix I) to see which databases are considered most useful to residents researching different topics and doing their homework.

When you start getting serious about finding the information you need, you begin to realize how enormous the information world is. This chapter presents a map of the information world that will help you visualize the many options you can choose from when seeking knowledge. We'll start with online commercial databases for text, numeric data, and images. "Commercial" means they charge the library an annual subscription fee or they charge your credit card if you search the database at the vendor's website without going through a library. Then we'll move on to freely available information of high quality. Some of these overlap; for example, a commercial database that charges real money may index U.S. congressional hearings, the highly informative transcripts of testimony by experts before a congressional committee investigating an issue. But those hearing transcripts are freely available on federal government websites. If you are

Table 9.1. Examples illustrating the terms database, database producer or publisher, database vendor, and platform brand name

Database	Database Producer or Publisher	Database Vendor	Platform Brand Name
General OneFile	Gale, Cengage Learning	Gale, Cengage Learning	Gale PowerSearch
MEDLINE	National Library of Medicine	Wolters Kluwer	OvidSP
PsycINFO	American Psychological Association	EBSCO	EBSCOhost

accustomed to the commercial database search platform, and you have free-to-you access via a library, you might as well use the commercial option. But if you're on your own, it's good to know there's a free alternative.

To begin, let's distinguish among the terms "database," "database producer" or "publisher," "database vendor," and "platform brand name." Table 9.1 provides three examples to help you learn the distinctions.

General OneFile indexes around thirteen thousand "titles," which includes magazines, newspapers, NPR radio transcripts, broadcast news, and whole encyclopedias. All of those resources are issued by a wide variety of producers and publishers. The Gale, Cengage Learning company arranges with each one to include its publications and broadcasts in the General OneFile database, and Gale (for short) is the publisher of the database itself. In this case Gale both creates and sells access to the database. And its brand name for the platform, including the search system and the interface, is Gale PowerSearch. Another database on the Gale PowerSearch platform is Academic OneFile. If you know how to search one, you know how to search the other.

The second example in the table, MEDLINE, is produced by a federal government agency, the National Library of Medicine, and it indexes sophisticated medical research published in scholarly journals. A big international information company, Wolters Kluwer, is one of the vendors that sells access to the database. The Wolters Kluwer brand name for its platform is OvidSP.

The third example is the PsycINFO database, created by a professional organization, the American Psychological Association, which has an agreement with the EBSCO company to sell access to the database on its EBSCO-host platform. The APA has an agreement with at least one of EBSCO's competitors, ProQuest, a name used for the vendor itself and for its platform. EBSCO, like its competitor Wolters Kluwer, also offers MEDLINE on the EBSCOhost platform. If you know how to use MEDLINE on the EBSCOhost platform, you'll know how to use PsychINFO on the EBSCOhost platform. The search engine will function the same way, and the look and feel of the interface will be familiar. The databases themselves have a few distinctive features because they cover different subject areas, but knowing the features of the search engine and where to find features and filters on the search and results screens will help you get your work done faster.

The advantage is that once you are familiar with a particular vendor's interface and search engine, you can apply that knowledge to the different databases offered by that vendor. At the same time, if you're used to searching MEDLINE on the EBSCOhost platform, it may take a little while to adjust to the different look and functionality of the OvidSP platform, but at least you'll know the database well enough to gauge whether your results look right. When you use open-access databases and repositories, the search engines may be less sophisticated, the interfaces less predictable, and the content not so obvious, all of which may slow you down a bit at first.

But let's get back to terminology. It's important to use the terms correctly and precisely to avoid confusion. Here's the deal: EBSCO is not a database. If you've been searching for something for a while and are not having much luck, you may decide to contact a librarian for help. If you say, "I've been using EBSCO and I can't find any articles on my topic," what have you actually told her? The library subscribes to five different databases on the EBSCOhost platform provided by the database vendor EBSCO. Maybe you've been searching MEDLINE when you should have been searching PsycINFO. In other words, you should always know which database you're searching. Sounds obvious, but when the search interface for one database looks identical to the interface for another database, it pays to slow down and check the screen to see precisely which database you're in, especially if you go to a physical library and sit down at a computer someone else was just using.

COMMERCIAL DATABASES

Many newspapers and magazines have websites at which you can read some articles for free. But most of the articles can only be read by paying for a subscription or ponying up a per-article fee. If you are looking for articles on a topic, it's costly and time-consuming to go to each newspaper or magazine website, do a search, and then pay for articles with your credit card. It's much more efficient to use a database to find articles on your topic in the hundreds or thousands of periodicals the database indexes.

Instead of going to a magazine website and hoping there's something on your topic, you can use a database accessible from a library. You can go to a town or state library's website and use the databases it subscribes to as a service to local residents. Or you can go to a college or university website and use the databases it subscribes to as a service to students and faculty. As part of their subscription, libraries agree to make the databases available only to their clientele, so when you try to use a database on the library's website, you'll have to log in with your library card, student/faculty ID card, or, at a state library website, your zip code. If you don't have a library card or you're not a student or faculty member at a university, you may want to check with the library to see if you can use the databases without any ID if you go to the physical library. Some allow that, while others require you to use your library card or student/faculty ID to log in whether you're physically in the library or elsewhere.

If using a library database isn't an option, there's always Google Scholar—which I like to think of as Google's smarter sister—at http://scholar.google.com/. Google Scholar is a search engine for academic literature, including articles in all kinds of scholarly journals. When Google Scholar finds an article on your topic, you may have two choices for accessing the full text of the article. Google Scholar may give you a link to the journal's website, where you may have to pay to get a copy of the whole article. Or, in maybe half the results, you might see a link off to the right that provides a free version of the article. Intrigued? Read on.

FREE RESOURCES

Any physical library offers "free" information; go right in and start browsing books and periodicals on the shelves or use the library catalog or one of the commercial databases to find information on a topic of interest. Of course, these aren't free to the library, but for you they are. The Internet in general offers free information of every description, much of it self-published and not subjected to the scrutiny of professional editors or librarians. On the Internet, though, are services that do carefully select the material they make available for free, as a traditional library does, and this section introduces you to the best of them. The web offers plenty of user-generated content sites, such as youtube.com and flickr.com, that host videos and images uploaded by the creators and copyright holders of those videos and images. (And sometimes by fans who don't actually have the right to upload them; if they're caught, they'll be told to take the illegal work down.) A lot of universities, colleges, and other institutions have YouTube channels, Flickr accounts, and space on similar sites at which they provide lectures, lessons, and historical images of great potential use for research projects. To find them, use the site's search box and input an institution's name.

There are two broad categories of free information: the public domain and open access to copyrighted work. It helps to know a bit about copyright to understand what makes these categories distinct.

Currently in the United States, any original expression—such as fiction or nonfiction, photographs, or scripts—is protected by copyright as soon as it's in a fixed form—on paper, in an e-mail, uploaded to a website—even if the creator doesn't register it with the U.S. Copyright Office. Under the current law, the work is protected for the lifespan of the individual creator/copyright holder plus seventy years. The period is even longer for companies. One of the main reasons commercial databases charge money to use them involves copyright. Publications are under copyright protection, which means only the copyright holder has the right to reproduce them and distribute them (among other things). Database creators must have a legal agreement with the publisher of the periodicals the database indexes to make articles from those periodicals available, and database creators pay for the privilege.

Once the copyright term ends, the work enters the public domain, meaning anybody can copy it freely, distribute it, and publish it or excerpts of it without having to get anyone's permission or pay anyone else for the right to do so. Currently, books, articles, photographs, movies, and similar material published before the early 1920s are in the public domain. You may not have any use for old information like that, but a lot of it is still of interest. If you want to read classic books now in the public domain, for example, you can download digitized copies of them for free. Great resources include Project Gutenberg (http://www.gutenberg.org/), the HathiTrust Digital Library (http://www.hathitrust.org/), and the Internet Archive (https://archive.org/).

In addition, many older stories and articles are available to read from your home or mobile device without paying a dime. A great resource is JSTOR (http://www.jstor.org/). Go right to the "advanced search" form, where you can use the date range box to limit results to the free public-domain material by inputting *1923* in the date range **to** box. You can leave the **from** box empty or fill in a year of your choice, as long as it's before 1923. For later work still under copyright, you can use your credit card or PayPal account to purchase articles, or you can use JSTOR through an academic library for free. Alternatively, you can access up to three free articles a month when you sign up with JSTOR's Register and Read program at http://about.jstor.org/rr.

Another database providing free access to more than two million of its articles is HighWire, a service of Stanford University. The search screen at http://highwire.stanford.edu/cgi/search helps you discover work on your topic, and if you register (free) with the service, you'll be able to use customizable tools such as having alerts sent to your e-mail whenever another article on your topic is added to the database.

Some material skips the copyright term altogether and starts life in the public domain. Almost any information created at the expense of the U.S. government by federal employees is in the public domain, not including the cool data kept secret for national security reasons. Since the federal government is one of the largest publishers in the world, that's a lot of authoritative information you can have for free. Why is being able to find government information so important? Well, when people are more knowledgeable about their government, they can make informed choices and, more and more, they can fully participate in the growing e-government phenomenon. But it goes beyond that.

Simply put, the U.S. government is interested in almost everything. And the government tends to make available to its citizens an astonishing array of information resources on a mind-boggling number of topics. Students with papers to write, elderly folks wondering about how to protect themselves from identity theft, parents worried about a toy recall, college students planning a trip abroad—all of them and more can find useful information from the federal government at no charge. No need to turn habitually to the commercial databases or your favorite web search engine when you find so much for free from government websites, if you know where and how to search. The best place to begin is the U.S. government's official web portal, http://www.usa.gov/, where you can use the search box at the top of the home page or scroll down to browse the links to agencies, topics, services, and state and local governments. If you are helping children learn, or if you're still young at heart, you should visit the portal for kids at http://kids.usa.gov/.

Federal websites have proliferated, and you can find them using the USA. gov portal. You can go straight to the ones that meet your information needs. Examples include FedStats (http://fedstats.sites.usa.gov/) for statistics on a wide variety of topics, and "the home of the U.S. Government's open data," http://www.data.gov/. If you want to follow what the U.S. Congress is doing, go to https://www.congress.gov/, and if you want to be aware of and even comment on a regulation a government agency is proposing, visit http://www.regulations.gov/.

Beyond the public domain, some copyright-protected work is available at no charge on the Internet, thanks in large part to the open-access movement of the last couple of decades. Open-access repositories and databases contain current research articles published in scholarly periodicals. To read a research article in a journal, you have to pay the journal publisher for it or use a commercial database that provides the full text of the article. But if the author has deposited the article in his or her university's repository or in a repository elsewhere that is dedicated to the subject the author researches, that copy can be freely found, downloaded, and read. It may be a preprint, the version the author wrote before the journal's staff edited it, it might be the PDF from the journal publisher, or it may be yet another version. But it's almost always a satisfactory substitute for the fee-based version. Notice that link over to the right of some of your results in Google Scholar? That may be the link that takes you to the free copy in the institutional or subject-based repository.

Two freely available databases help you find open-access journals, the Directory of Open Access Journals (DOAJ), at http://doaj.org/, and the Directory of Open Access Repositories (OpenDOAR), at http://opendoar.org/. The DOAJ lists more than ten thousand journals published in more than one hundred countries and indexes the articles from more than six thousand of them. The home page offers a search box with checkboxes under it that let you limit your results to journals, or to articles in the journals, or both. If you want to find open-access journals in your major or career field whose issues you can browse through, check the journals box. If you want articles on a topic and don't care what journals they're in, check the articles box.

The DOAR lists more than twenty-five hundred repositories worldwide, and you can find them by subject, place, and other factors using the search form at http://opendoar.org/find.php. You can search the contents of the repositories using DOAR's search box at http://opendoar.org/search.php. Repositories often rely on busy researchers to self-deposit, in other words, to get around to logging in and uploading their work to the repository. Unlike commercial databases, which make it their business to collect and index research articles systematically, repositories may be a bit hit-or-miss. At the same time, if you know a university has a highly ranked medical school, for example, and you're looking for the latest research on a particular illness, you may want to search that university's repository, where you may find important reports and articles absolutely free. Combine that with a search at USA.gov, and you may be able to compile some useful information about an illness (or other matters of interest to you) without ever leaving home or pulling out your credit card.

Many authors and other copyright holders have decided that copyright is too restrictive, and they've started giving away some of their exclusive rights guaranteed by the copyright law. They are part of the Creative Commons (CC) movement, which has developed six different licenses that give away some or most of the copyright holder's exclusive rights. You can find CC-licensed material that allows you to read work for free and do other things with it, such as add a copy of the work to your own website, as long as you credit the original author. Much of this material is research-oriented.

On the Google Advanced Search form at http://www.google.com/advanced_search, scroll down to the last box, labeled **usage rights**, and select one of the choices, such as **free to use or share**. The usage rights choices are based on the different kinds of CC licenses that people might attach to their copyrighted work to give away some of the exclusive rights normally retained by the copyright holder. The image site Flickr offers an advanced search form link (viewable after you do your first search) that allows you to limit results to those in which the photographers or videographers have published their work under a CC license.

The Creative Commons website offers a search box at http://search .creativecommons.org/ that lets you search different services, such as You-Tube for videos and SoundCloud for music, to find material freely available for you to enjoy and even reuse in your own original creations.

Rounding out our tour of the information world are digital libraries, at which you can find public domain and CC-licensed material. An extremely cool place to start is the Internet Archive (https://archive.org/), a nonprofit organization that gives you free access to old television commercials, radio news programs, public domain books, recently published open-access books issued under CC licenses, software and classic computer games, and other kinds of things. You can find more than 450 billion archived web pages using the Internet Archives Wayback Machine, which searches by URL. What did Verizon's first web page look like? Now you know how to find it. Fun fact: it included a tip on how to pronounce the company's name.

Another excellent resource is the National Science Digital Library (https:// nsdl.oercommons.org/). Anyone of almost any age who wants to understand a topic related to the sciences, technology, engineering, or math can find a lot of good help at NSDL. The search system lets you limit your results to specific subject areas, your educational level, and the kind of material you want, such as data or lectures, among other things. This is user-created content at its finest, with many researchers contributing lesson plans, clearly illustrated explanations of physical phenomena, and multimedia presentations.

Other digital collections focused on geography and history are available from many different states. The U.S. Library of Congress provides a list at http://www.loc.gov/rr/program/bib/statememory/. Another way to find such collections is to use your favorite web search engine to search *"digital library"* being sure to include the quotation marks so the phrase is searched (rather than the two separate words). And of course you can toss in another keyword to limit your results to particular kinds of digital libraries; try adding a term such as *children*, for instance, or *art*.

The world of information turns out to be bigger than most of us can imagine. If you're stuck in a Google rut, be forewarned that you might find a new favorite database and get stuck in, say, a General OneFile rut. When a database has a user-friendly interface and gives you easy access to huge numbers of articles published about something you're interested in, it's easy to keep going back to it for more, perhaps on a different topic. I encourage you to think a bit more strategically, however. For important projects especially—a term paper, a business report, your group's advocacy video for a policy change, the need to understand a medical diagnosis and treatment—using different information resources well gives you the power of knowledge. Combining the results from a commercial database with the free research reports found via Google Scholar and the latest data from a government agency can help you satisfy your curiosity and make your case.

CHAPTER 10

Browsing and Searching

The word "browsing" might make you think of the way you click on photos of products at your favorite online retailer. Or it might make you think of what a lot of people call "surfing the web." But in the search industry, browsing means something specific. It refers to reading and selecting from a list of options arranged in a particular way. If you've ever done a search, you've browsed. You have browsed the list of results to decide which ones to use.

You can also browse without searching. For example, you may use a web portal that has information organized by subject, with the subjects commonly listed in alphabetical order. You click on the category you're interested in, and you're given another alphabetical list, this time of subcategories. Some people call this "drilling down" through the links to eventually arrive at the information you want. But we call it browsing, because it involves skimming an organized list and choosing from it.

In contrast, searching involves inputting terms and letting the retrieval system find the terms for you. Almost always, when we're seeking information, we begin with a keyword search, as Google has trained us to do. But it's worth thinking about the advantages of browsing so you can make informed decisions about whether to search or to browse, depending on the circumstances. Most of the time, you'll combine searching and browsing to locate what you want.

THE BROWSING ADVANTAGE

Browsing refers to reading or skimming a list. Usually the list is in some order. It may be alphabetical by last name, as in the residential phone book. It may be chronological, as in a time line of historical events. In the case of traditional bibliographic database results, it may be last-in, first-out, meaning that the items most recently indexed appear highest in the list. With a web search engine, it may be in rank order by "relevance" as calculated by a proprietary algorithm (a set of instructions to the search engine regarding which results to present and in what order). In a directory or portal, such as USA.gov, it may be in broad categories of subjects that branch into narrower and narrower topics. In the latter case, browsing by topic can help you clarify your information needs as you go along. Browsing can help you discover new resources you didn't suspect existed. When your map of the information world is sketchy, browsing can fill in the gaps, leading you step by step to needed resources. You can see where you're going and, if you find yourself clicking down a blind alley, you can back up and take a different route.

In contrast, when you search instead of browsing, you don't see what's happening as the search system finds your words in its indexes, retrieves the linked records, and then presents a list of brief results for you to evaluate. With browsing, you learn about topics as you go along by seeing how the information is organized and presented. You get a sense of the scope of a topic by moving from its broadest category to its narrower subcategories.

Let's use USA.gov, the federal government's web portal, to see how beneficial browsing can be. The home page offers a search box at the top, but the middle of the page lists categories you can browse. They are in alphabetical order from left to right, beginning with the A–Z index to agencies of the U.S. government, as figure 10.1 shows.

If you click on the category labeled **Jobs and Unemployment**, you're taken to a page with seven subcategories, beginning with a link labeled **For**

Figure 10.1. Browsable topics offered in the middle of the USA.gov home page.

Business Owners and ending with one labeled **Volunteer Opportunities**. If you click on the **Looking for a New Job** link, you will go to a page offering two options, one for federal job hunting and one with general job hunting help. Either choice will lead to yet more links offering more specific information, about writing a resume, finding an apprenticeship opportunity, deciding on a career, and similar topics.

Browsing is an option in seemingly unlikely places. When you use your favorite web search engine, an entry from *Wikipedia* often appears at the top of the list of results. If you visit the English-language *Wikipedia* home page at http://en.wikipedia.org/wiki/Main_Page, you'll see that the encyclopedia is browsable by topic. If you select the first topic, **Arts**, you'll be taken to a page that *Wikipedia* refers to as the Arts Portal. Scroll down it a bit to find browsable subcategories. Clicking on one of the subcategories, **Censorship in the arts**, takes you to a page listing three additional topics, linking to *Wikipedia* entries on film censorship, censorship of music, and video game censorship. The page lists all of the *Wikipedia* items that address censorship, including links to the entries on comedians Lenny Bruce, George Carlin, and Richard Pryor, for example. Browsing certainly isn't the customary way to interact with *Wikipedia*, but it may be helpful when you have to decide on a topic for a research paper and you're looking for inspiration, or in other cases when you need a little bit of guidance.

ERIC DATABASE

A freely accessible database that indexes education-related research and publications is ERIC (the Education Resources Information Center). The federal Department of Education's Institute of Education Sciences maintains the database at http://eric.ed.gov/. In addition, ERIC is available from several database vendors, who overlay the database with their own search

Figure 10.2. The search box on the home page of the openly accessible ERIC database.

interfaces and systems. We're going to use the free version on the Department of Education's website to explore the practical realities of basic search techniques in a huge database with a Google-like search engine and as a way to see how browsing and searching work together (see figure 10.2).

A Few Things to Know First

The ERIC database contains more than one million records going back to the 1960s. Everything in the database relates to education in some way. There are two kinds of material indexed in ERIC: published articles from scholarly journals and other kinds of publications that ERIC refers to as "non-journal sources." These include reports from government agencies, nonprofit organizations, research institutes, individuals, and other entities. Most of the non-journal material is available in full text from within the ERIC database. Many of the journal articles are not; you might see a link for many of the journal articles in your results, but the links take you to the publisher website, where you'll have to pay for the article. If you use ERIC via a library that provides access to it on a commercial platform, you'll most likely see links that provide the full text at no charge to you.

The free version of ERIC has a stripped-down interface much like Google's. There's no advanced search form to fill in. A tiny link to the right of the search box offers helpful tips that explain how to limit searches to fields (for example) within the single search box on the home page. The advanced search tips are worth consulting if you're going to do a lot of ERIC searching.

The search page has two tabs above the search box. The default tab is "collection," and any keywords you type in the box will search the **Collection** of material indexed in ERIC. The other tab leads to the **Thesaurus**, the list of subject descriptors for the field of education. You can search or browse the thesaurus to find the preferred terms for your topics and thus avoid having to think up all the synonyms for your topics. Once you learn the correct descriptor from the thesaurus, you can search the collection and limit the term to the subject descriptor field by inputting the field label followed by a colon and then the descriptor itself, for example, *descriptor:volunteers*.

What follows is a series of search strategies, from simple to more sophisticated. Although the search page and system mimic Google, the results page offers much more information to help you select useful-looking material and help you narrow your results.

We'll begin with a search using the keyword *bullying*, as seen in figure 10.3.

As you can see in the example, the column to the right lists the results as brief records, including the title, authors, source, beginning of the abstract,

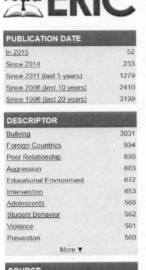

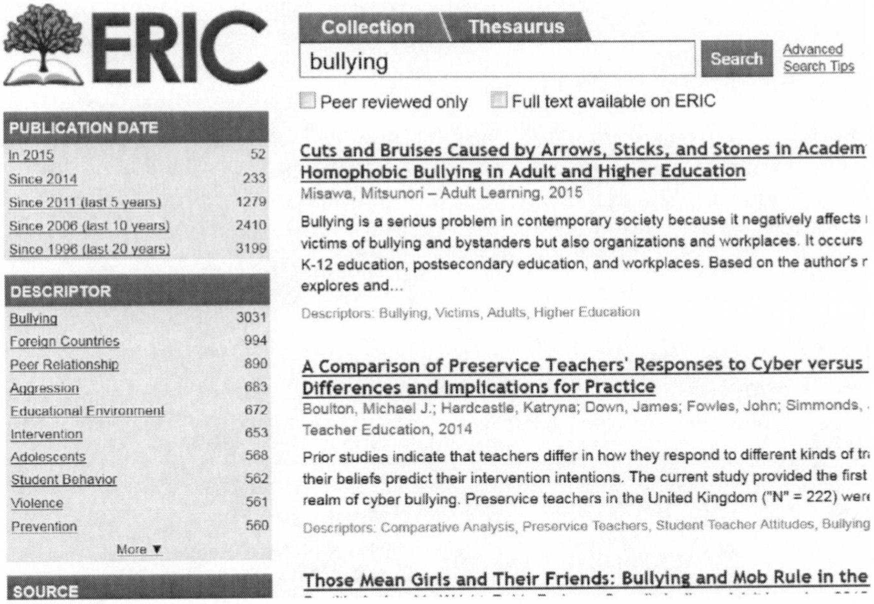

Collection \ **Thesaurus**

bullying   Search   Advanced
                                              Search Tips

☐ Peer reviewed only   ☐ Full text available on ERIC

PUBLICATION DATE

In 2015	52
Since 2014	233
Since 2011 (last 5 years)	1279
Since 2006 (last 10 years)	2410
Since 1996 (last 20 years)	3199

DESCRIPTOR

Bullying	3031
Foreign Countries	994
Peer Relationship	890
Aggression	683
Educational Environment	672
Intervention	653
Adolescents	568
Student Behavior	562
Violence	561
Prevention	560

More ▼

SOURCE

Cuts and Bruises Caused by Arrows, Sticks, and Stones in Academ
Homophobic Bullying in Adult and Higher Education
Misawa, Mitsunori – Adult Learning, 2015

Bullying is a serious problem in contemporary society because it negatively affects i
victims of bullying and bystanders but also organizations and workplaces. It occurs
K-12 education, postsecondary education, and workplaces. Based on the author's r
explores and...

Descriptors: Bullying, Victims, Adults, Higher Education

A Comparison of Preservice Teachers' Responses to Cyber versus
Differences and Implications for Practice
Boulton, Michael J.; Hardcastle, Katryna; Down, James; Fowles, John; Simmonds, .
Teacher Education, 2014

Prior studies indicate that teachers differ in how they respond to different kinds of tr
their beliefs predict their intervention intentions. The current study provided the first
realm of cyber bullying. Preservice teachers in the United Kingdom ("N" = 222) wer

Descriptors: Comparative Analysis, Preservice Teachers, Student Teacher Attitudes, Bullying

Those Mean Girls and Their Friends: Bullying and Mob Rule in the

Figure 10.3. Keyword search for *bullying* in the ERIC database, with results listed under the search box and filters shown to the left.

and first few subject descriptors assigned to each item. You can click on any title to see the full record with the complete abstract.

The column on the left side of the screen tells us more about the results overall, with total results by time period, subject descriptors, source (journal name), authors' names, type of publication, educational level discussed in the publication, and the publication's intended audience. Each item on the left is a link, so if you want to see only the fifty-two articles published in 2015, a single click will show them.

ERIC gives you lots of help with its left-side filters. Notice that when you are checking the totals in the left-side column, you are browsing. In the Publication Date category, you are browsing in time period order, from the current year to the accumulated total during the past twenty years. The other categories are in rank order from most to least number of results. You can use these filters as they're intended, for refining your results. But you can also use them the same way you use other kinds of browsing activity, to learn more about your topic and ultimately to devise better search strategies.

Because the ERIC search system on the open web is more like Google than it is like a commercial database search engine, it works well if you type in your search terms without using Boolean operators or quotation marks.

A relevance algorithm working behind the scenes retrieves the results that include your terms repeatedly in the title, author, source, abstract, and descriptor fields. For example, the search *teachers bullying harassment* yields 145 results. Again, you can use the left-side filters to select from those items and the peer-reviewed checkbox to show research articles in scholarly journals. And you can use the full-text-only checkbox if you want the actual publications, even if they aren't quite as relevant as some of the results that only include references and abstracts for free in the ERIC database.

Nothing's easier than inputting the first keywords that come to mind, limiting to full text, and then selecting from the small set of results retrieved. A search system programmed to facilitate that approach assumes you want fewer results. Otherwise, you might be overwhelmed by the large numbers of results you get when you search the web or a database like ERIC. If you have a nagging worry that you may not be finding everything relevant to your topic, here are some extra steps you can take.

One of the most common ways to search is to use the Boolean *and* operator to include a different concept. If you are interested in the role of school counselors in cases of bullying, you can do a simple search: *bullying school counselors*. If you use the *and* between *bullying* and *school counselors*, you'll get the same number of results, which means that the space between words functions like a Boolean *and*. If you remember your grade-school math lessons, you know that two plus three equals three plus two, and the logic is the same with the Boolean *and*. Whether you type *bullying school counselors* or *school counselors bullying* or *school bullying counselors*, you'll get the same results. Again, as with many search engines, the space between two terms acts as a Boolean *and*.

In this case, it's better to put the phrase in quotation marks—*"school counselors"*—to make sure the system finds the phrase. Again, it doesn't matter if we input *bullying "school counselors"* or *"school counselors" bullying*. Either search yields one hundred results. We eliminated the forty-five results that contained the word *school* and the word *counselors* but not next to each other in that order, in other words, as a phrase.

Although the web-based ERIC system wasn't designed to use Boolean operators, you can use *or* to find synonyms, such as *bullying or harassment*. As with most search engines, ERIC on the web lets you limit your terms to different fields. If you know a particular author's work, you can use the field label *author:* right before the author's name, as in *author:cheryl knott*. It's more likely you're looking for articles on a topic, though. You can limit your keywords to the *title:* field. Keep in mind that titles tend to be rather short and may not include your keyword even though the article does. So you might want to try limiting your keyword to the *abstract:* instead. The abstract is a short summary of the article, and it includes more words than the title does, so it increases the likelihood that your keyword is mentioned.

If your topic is a phrase, do include the quotation marks, as in the following search:

abstract:"school counselors"

Even better, use descriptors instead of your everyday natural language keywords. Doing a quick search like *bullying or harassment* can teach you what the preferred subject terms for your topic are. Look in the left-side column under the heading **Descriptor** and click on the one that fits best to see results that are tagged with that descriptor.

Before you begin searching, ERIC's handy **Thesaurus** tab above the search box on the home page can help you discover the preferred terms, as well as broader, narrower, and related terms, for your topics. Always check the **Include Synonyms** box when you search the ERIC thesaurus. When you search *school counselors* in the thesaurus, you'll see that it has been the preferred subject term since 1980 (before 1980, the preferred term was *counselors*, which is now recommended as the broader term to use). Two of the related terms are *school counseling* and *school psychologists*. If you look up bullying, you'll see that it's the correct descriptor, with a broader term being *antisocial behavior* and related terms being *aggression, social distance,* and *violence*.

Let's browse the thesaurus. When you're on the **Thesaurus** tab, click on the **Browse Thesaurus** link to the right of the search box. You'll be offered an alphabetical list of broad subjects. Click on one, such as *Social Problems*, and you'll be taken to another alphabetical list, this time of subtopics. You can find *Bullying* here, along with drug abuse, plagiarism, and school vandalism, among other issues. If you click on *Bullying*, you'll go to the same page we found when we searched the thesaurus for *bullying*. If you don't want to combine that term with any other terms, you can click on the handy **Search collection using this descriptor** link to go straight to the list of results, all the items in the database tagged with the subject term *Bullying*, along with all the usual filters on the left side of the screen.

Whether you search or browse the thesaurus, you can learn a lot about your topic and the language scholars use to describe it. The thesaurus can help you think more carefully about your topic and decide, for example, whether you are actually trying to find material about how school psychologists rather than counselors are dealing with student-on-student bullying. Or you might discover that your real concerns involve sexual harassment rather than bullying. Either way, the thesaurus can be checked quickly to confirm your terms or help you find the correct ones for your topic.

Our natural language, the language we use to speak and write, can cause problems for us when we are trying to retrieve information. When you are looking for articles about cancer, if you search only for *cancer* you might miss some relevant and important works. So it's a good idea to use your Boolean operator to search for *cancer or malignancy or "malignant tumors" or* . . . well, who knows how many you'll have to include to make sure you are being thorough?

Then there's the problem of words that are spelled alike but have different meanings. When you are looking for articles about china, how do you avoid getting articles about China? That's why we have what's known in the information business as controlled vocabularies. A controlled vocabulary selects one preferred term for each topic. For example, the preferred term in a controlled vocabulary may be *motion pictures*. When a person or an automated system is indexing an article, the preferred term *motion pictures* will be added to each record for an article about motion pictures. The author of the article may have used the term *films* or *movies* or both, but you don't have to guess what the author did. You can simply search the subject descriptor field for the preferred term and find all the relevant material about that topic. The preferred terms are listed in a thesaurus. This is not like Roget's thesaurus or the thesaurus in your word processing software. Usually devoted to a single broad subject, such as psychology or education or architecture, this kind of thesaurus tells which are the correct terms for your topic. If you look up a term that's not the correct preferred descriptor, the thesaurus will refer you to the correct term.

You can learn a lot about a subject by consulting its thesaurus, as we did with the education thesaurus in ERIC. Now that we know the subject descriptors for our topics, we can return to the **Collection** tab and use the field label *descriptor:* to craft a better search, such as:

descriptor:bullying descriptor:"school counselors"

That yields seventy-six results. Remember a few paragraphs back, when we searched *bullying "school counselors"* and got one hundred results? The twenty-five that were left out of our descriptor search were items that mentioned bullying and school counselors but were not about those topics, at least not sufficiently about them to tag them with the bullying and school counselors descriptors. Descriptors are always added later, after an analysis of the item reveals what it is about. They come in handy when a title and abstract discuss "the bullied child" without ever mentioning your keyword *bullying*. By tagging that item with the descriptor *bullying*, the system is making sure you find it. A keyword-based search looks for records using those keywords, while a descriptor-based search looks for records tagged with those descriptors. Think about how much time you saved yourself by eliminating those twenty-five casual mentions of your keywords with your descriptor-based search. You did not have to look at each of those twenty-five results to decide they weren't relevant to your topic; the search system did that for you.

The eric.ed.edu system doesn't use the Boolean operator *not*. But you can eliminate terms using the minus sign (the hyphen). The ERIC help page suggests the search

bullying -gay

to eliminate articles that focus on bullying of gay people. I never suggest using the *not* operator or the minus sign in that way, because it could easily delete results you'd like to see. For example, it would eliminate all the articles that mention bullying of both gay and straight teens, simply because you told the system to leave out everything with the word *gay* in it. If your research focuses on straight teens, some of the eliminated material that discusses gay and straight teens might be of interest, but you won't even know it exists. Minusing out a term often minuses out a topic, which is hardly ever a good idea when you're doing serious research.

The Boolean operator *not* (or the minus sign) does have its place, however. It's great for eliminating certain kinds of material, such as when the search engine allows you to *not* out all the records for a type of document, such as book reviews. Free-access ERIC doesn't have a document type field index, so that won't work there, but you can eliminate a particular source, such as a journal you read all the time. Furthermore, *not* (the word or the minus sign) can be used to give you an idea of what's missing from your search results. This search

bullying -descriptor:bullying

will show you all the results that mention *bullying* but were not tagged with the descriptor *bullying* (see table 10.1).

There were 260 records in the database in which bullying was mentioned in the title or abstract but not in the descriptor field. In other words, the individuals indexing those 260 items didn't think they were sufficiently about bullying to merit the addition of the subject descriptor *bullying* to

Table 10.1. Use of minus sign to calculate the number of results using *bullying* as a keyword, but not sufficiently about bullying to be tagged with the descriptor

Search	Results
bullying	3,291
descriptor:bullying	3,031
Bullying -descriptor:bullying	260

each one's database record. I might skim those 260 items to get a sense of what I'm leaving out when I search by descriptor only. That's not something you need to do every time you search, but it can help you convince yourself that it's okay to only search with the descriptor or, conversely, to decide that you need to cast a wider net by searching the term as a natural-language keyword. It might be especially helpful if you are researching a new topic, in which case the descriptor has been added to the thesaurus and used to tag articles only recently. Eliminating the recently tagged material might help you see quickly what the earlier literature covered and what the earlier descriptors were. And it might convince you that you should search this new topic with keywords instead of descriptors to make sure you're not missing some useful publications.

When you search eric.ed.gov, you're going right to the source of the database, so it's the most up-to-date version. It may take a while for the latest material to make it into the ERIC database when it's served up by a vendor on a commercial platform. Some vendors update databases only monthly or perhaps weekly. If you are working on a hot topic, you might want to stick with the free version of ERIC to make sure you're finding the most recently added information.

CHAPTER 11

Evaluating and Managing Search Results

Once you start mastering the art and science of online searching, relevant results will start to accumulate. A number of methods for managing your references are available. Some are built in to the commercial databases we've been using, and some are add-ons that you can download and use for free. Using these techniques will help you

- easily update results when new material is published,
- keep your different search projects organized, and
- cite your sources correctly.

After you search, you're taken to a results page that offers you a list of brief records from which to choose. Each of the article titles in the list of records is a link to the full record, which gives all the information you'll need to judge whether the article is relevant to your research. As you evaluate the list, here are some things to consider.

- Read the title. Does it use words you understand readily? Do words in the title suggest to you the article will discuss your topic in sufficient detail for your purposes?
- Can you tell how long the article is? Some databases such as General and Academic OneFile tell you the word count; others will give you the number of pages or the page numbers where the article appears in the magazine or journal. If you need a detailed article, you may want to skip the ones that are one page long or under 500 words.
- How recent is the work? For historical topics this may not matter, but for many topics you'll want the most up-to-date publications you can find.

- Read the summary of the article if one is provided. You may have to click on the title to see the full record with the entire summary. Writing such summaries, or abstracts as they are commonly called, is an art form in and of itself, but a good one truly summarizes the article, which is key to your decision to download the full text or track it down in the library.
- Descriptors or subject tags added to each record are worth skimming, because they tell you what the article is about in a few words or phrases.

Of course your evaluation of your first or even second set of results may lead you to believe you need to revise your search strategy a bit. But sooner or later you'll craft the perfect query for your search project, and then you'll pick the most relevant items from the list of great results. If you have a few items, it's easy to click on each link to the full text, usually in the form of a PDF file, and save it to your hard drive or print it out.

For a project that's more involved, or for research that's ongoing, the commercial databases give you additional choices to help you stay organized and efficient. These include sending the list of results to your e-mail, exporting results in a comma-delimited form that makes it easy to load them into your favorite spreadsheet program, and saving them to a reference management program. For ongoing research, many commercial platforms allow you to save your search strategy so you can easily find new publications as soon as they are added to the database. You usually have to sign up for a free account, which gives you space to store your search strategies and results. Let's look at two different platforms to see the kinds of things you can do with sets of results.

GALE CENGAGE PLATFORM

As we've seen, after you've input a search, a list of results is displayed along with some options, usually on the left of the screen, for filtering and refining your results. Most systems allow you to sort the list of results in different ways. The Gale Cengage platform displays results in order of publication date, with the most recent work at the top of the list. A small **Sort by** box above and to the right of the results list offers a pull-down menu for changing the order to ascending publication date so that your results will appear in a chronological arrangement from oldest to newest. You can choose to sort results by relevance, with relevance being calculated by a proprietary algorithm that works behind the scenes.

Gale Cengage offers free accounts that allow you to save search strategies and results. In the top navigation bar, which is green, click on the **Sign In** link, then the **New User** link, to fill out the form requesting an account.

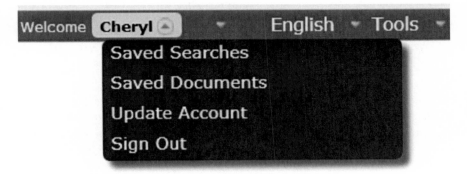

Figure 11.1. Options to reuse searches and documents when signed in to a Gale Cengage database. © Gale, a part of Cengage Learning, Inc. Reproduced by permission www.cengage .com/permissions.

Once you have an account, you can sign in to access your saved searches and results, as shown in figure 11.1.

Both General and Academic OneFile allow you to save search results by clicking on the link labeled **Save this search**, in the **Tools** box to the right of your list of brief-record results. When you click on the **Save this search** link, you'll be prompted to provide a file name to save it under, and you'll see a checkbox for **Create Search Alert**. A search alert e-mails you when new results matching your saved search are available in the database, on a daily, weekly, or monthly schedule of your choosing.

To save documents, use the checkboxes at the beginning of each brief record in your list to select the ones you want. If you're logged in to your account on the site, the full records, including the full text if available, will automatically be saved for you.

If you click on the title of an item in your brief-records list of results, you'll be shown the full record, which often includes the full text of the article as well as a link to the full article as a PDF file. If you display the article PDF, you can download it to your computer. On the full-record page are additional options for working with results. A small **Listen** button above the text lets you hear a reading of the article, and a box on the right side of the text has a link for downloading the mp3 audio file of the reading to your computer. Anytime you download a file, whether it's text, PDF, audio, or another format, the system automatically gives it a name. When you choose to "Save as" you should go ahead and change the filename to something you'll recognize later. A good way to stay organized is to use a consistent pattern of naming, such as authorname_yearpublished_titlekeyword.pdf, of course substituting the last name of the article's author, the year the article was published, and a distinctive keyword from the title of the article. You may want to create a folder on your hard drive to save all your material related to a single research project, giving the folder a name that reflects the research topic.

If you are writing a report from the research material you're gathering, one of the most helpful features in the right-hand box is the link labeled **Citation Tools**. Clicking on it shows you how to cite the article in conformity with either the Modern Language Association (MLA) citation style or the American Psychological Association (APA) style. (There are other citation styles, but these are the two Gale Cengage uses to format your citations for you.) Citing your sources in conformity with a designated style is standard practice for a research report, whether you are turning it in for a course grade or submitting it to a scholarly journal for publication. You may need to double-check the formatting provided by the database platform with the style examples on the associations' websites, since these sometimes get out of sync.

In the same **Citation Tools** window is the option to export the citation to one of five reference management software programs. If you use one of those programs, you can have the database send the citation in the correct format so you can easily import it to whichever program you're using. You may own the software yourself, or you may use a library that provides access to one of these software packages. If you use the library's software, you'll need to register for a free account, at which you can store your bibliographies of sources, use them to write different papers, and change the citation styles as needed for different courses or different journals.

If you don't want to buy software or use the library's software, you can download a free open-source reference manager. A few are available, and one of the most popular is Zotero. When you choose to download a citation using the Gale Cengage **Citation Tool**, one of the choices is Zotero if you have downloaded and installed the Zotero program to your computer. Zotero makes things super easy, so you can click on the folder icon that Zotero adds to every URL address box when you're surfing the web and when you're searching a commercial database or an open-access repository via the web. Let's learn a bit more about this helpful citation manager.

ZOTERO

You can download the program for the Mac, Windows, and Linux operating systems at https://www.zotero.org/. You can download the version of Zotero that works with the Firefox browser, or you can download a stand-alone version. The Firefox version is recommended. Anytime you have a Firefox window open, you'll see its Z icon in the navigation bar, in the upper right of the screen. A handy manual explaining how to use the program will be downloaded as well.

Zotero organizes your citations into libraries. Each library is a file of citations that Zotero has saved from your various searches. To stay organized, you should create a library for each different research project and name them accordingly. You can manually type in citations if, for example, you've found a source cited in a book that you want to include. Each library is a bibliography of sources about your research topic.

A great time-saver is the Zotero add-in that you can use from within Word or LibreOffice. As you are writing your report, you can use the Zotero add-in to find an item in one of your libraries and add a citation to it in your report. Not only that, but Zotero will format the citation to conform to one of the many citation styles used by professional associations and scholarly journals. It can generate a bibliography of your citations for a list of references at the end of your report.

You can use Zotero to capture citations from the open web and from behind database paywalls. But let's take one more look at what features another commercial database platform offers for working with results. We've seen what our options are with Gale Cengage; now let's consider EBSCOhost.

EBSCOHOST

After you've logged in to one of the databases hosted by EBSCO via your local library, you'll see the search screen. At the top will be a blue navigation bar, and on its right-hand side is a link to **Sign In**. The first time you click on that link, you'll be able to register on the EBSCO site, and then you can use the username and password you specified to sign in each time. While you are signed in, you can save results to folders that can be used again the next time you sign in. You can set preferences for certain search and results features, such as whether you want the search system to autocomplete terms you start typing into the search boxes and what e-mail address you always want the system to use when you have a list of results sent to you.

Signing in lets you save search strategies so you can reuse them, and you can set up search alerts to run automatically, saving you the trouble of logging in and keying in repetitive searches. As figure 11.2 shows, my search for *cesar chavez and dolores huerta* in the Chicano Database yielded twenty-two results. Once you've conducted a search, use the **Share** feature above and to the right of the results list to save the results and/or the search strategy to a folder. You can use the **E-mail Alert** feature to command the search system to run that same search on a regular interval, such as monthly, and e-mail the results to you.

In some databases, EBSCO offers the option to create a journal alert, which e-mails you every time new issues of your selected journals are indexed and

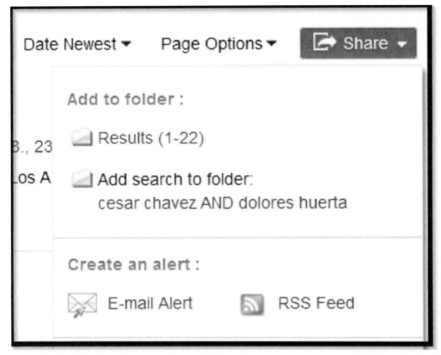

Figure 11.2. EBSCOhost Share features available from the results screen. © 2015 EBSCO Industries, Inc. Used with permission of EBSCO Information Services.

added to the database. To set up a journal alert, work from the **Publications** link in the blue navigation bar, as shown in figure 11.3.

Browse to the journal you want to create an alert for, check the box next to its title, and then click on the little icon to the right of the checkbox (see figure 11.4). A screen will open that allows you to specify which e-mail address to send alerts to, along with a few other options.

Figure 11.3. From the Academic Search Complete search screen, the Publications link in the navigation bar can be used to create a journal alert. © 2015 EBSCO Industries, Inc. Used with permission of EBSCO Information Services.

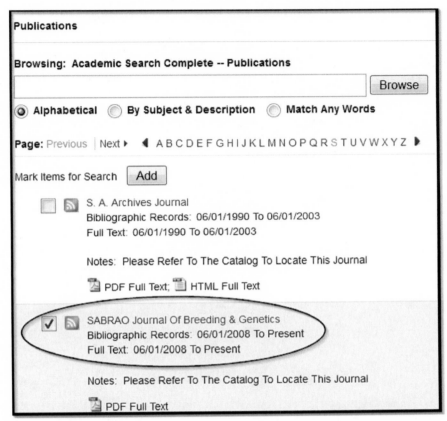

Figure 11.4. Journal alerts can be created from the Publications list in Academic Search Complete. © 2015 EBSCO Industries, Inc. Used with permission of EBSCO Information Services.

Successful searching doesn't end with a list of results. Evaluating, selecting, saving, using, and citing results are part of the process. Commercial databases are especially helpful when it comes to working with results. Their records include complete information about an article, book chapter, dissertation, or other item to help you evaluate whether the full text will serve your needs. And that complete information—author's name, title of the piece, publisher, and so forth—will come in handy when you want to cite the source of your information. Many commercial database vendors include instructions on how to cite sources in conformity with standard citation guides. For example, EBSCOhost's help screens include patterns to follow for citation styles designed by the American Psychological Association, the Modern Languages Association, and other professional and educational organizations. Students working on research papers will find it easier to meet their instructors' expectations for proper citation if they follow the style specified.

Students may be less interested in setting up search and journal alerts, but individuals in the workforce may find that staying up-to-date with the research literature in their field or industry gives them a competitive advantage. Alerting services can be especially helpful to a team of colleagues working on a project, and each person's e-mail address can be included so all team members receive new information at the same time. Once you feel comfortable with designing search strategies and deploying them, you can build on your knowledge by exploring the additional features available for working with results.

CHAPTER 12

Crowding Out the Experts

If you've worked your way through this book, you've probably had a moment that many of the students in my online searching courses experience, a moment when you asked yourself, "Why didn't I know all this already?" Even students who come into my courses with high levels of confidence regarding their web-search skills see that there's much more to explore, many resources not openly accessible, and many techniques for efficient and effective information retrieval.

You've picked up a lot of search tidbits in these chapters, and you've probably noticed on your own various features and functions that you have experimented with and plan to try again. In my opinion, the most important things for you to have learned are these:

1. Commercial databases indexing popular and scholarly articles, books, statistical reports, and other information are not free, but you can access many of them through your state, school, or public library.
2. Search techniques such as using the Boolean *and* to combine terms representing different concepts and the Boolean *or* to include synonyms for the same concept can help you retrieve the most relevant material, while lessening the likelihood of missing something on your topic.
3. Using a variety of resources such as a commercial index, an open-access repository, and a government website—all related to the subject of your research—can yield a balanced collection of material on your topic from different perspectives.
4. Retrieval isn't the same as relevance, no matter what Google's relevance-ranking algorithm would like you to believe, so always evaluate the sources you discover, checking the scope of their focus on your topic, the qualifications or credentials of the authors, the publication

123

date, the type of publication, and similar factors as you decide whether each item is relevant for your purposes.
5. Let search systems help you stay organized and up-to-date by registering for services that allow you to save search strategies and results, alert you to new material in your field, and help you cite the sources you use in reports and papers.

Does this mean you can never go back to plain old web searching? Well, no. But you are in a far better position now to make choices about how you find information, depending on your reasons for needing the information, your deadlines, and your motivations. You can still Google it. You can still crowd-source it, asking friends and followers on social media to answer a question you have or recommend a service you need. But now you can plan and execute a well-thought-out search strategy in huge databases fitted with sophisticated information organization and retrieval systems.

And perhaps at least as important as all that, you are now equipped with a vocabulary and a deeper understanding that will allow you to ask intelligent questions of the search experts at the library (or those independent entrepreneurs who establish their own information-brokering firms) when you are stumped.

May you find the information you need!

APPENDIX I

Databases Accessible from State Libraries or Other State Agencies

You can use commercial databases by visiting the state library in your state's capital city or a public library in the county, city, or town where you live. If you cannot visit the library, you can get free Internet access to commercial databases at the link below for your state, but you will need to input a library card number or other proof that you are a state resident entitled to use the databases. Florida and Kentucky allow remote access for state employees only.

Alabama Virtual Library: http://www.avl.lib.al.us/

Alaska State Library, SLED Databases: http://sled.alaska.edu/databases/az.html

Arizona State Library, Archives and Public Records, Databases: http://www.azlibrary.gov/dazl/databases

Arkansas State Library, Online Databases: http://www.library.arkansas.gov/references/Pages/OnlineDatabases.aspx

California State Library, Online Resources for State Government (and for anyone in the reading rooms): http://www.library.ca.gov/services/online-resources.html

Colorado: Access is available via university, college, K–12, and public libraries.

Connecticut State Library, A–Z Databases: http://libguides.ctstatelibrary.org/az.php

Delaware Division of Libraries, Delaware Libraries: http://lib.de.us/emedia/

Florida Division of Library and Information Services, Electronic Databases (remote access available to state employees; on-site access for others): http://dlis.dos.state.fl.us/cgi-bin/services

University System of Georgia, Galileo: http://www.galileo.usg.edu/
welcome/

Hawaii State Public Library System, Electronic Resources: http://www
.librarieshawaii.org/Serials/databases.html

Idaho Commission for Libraries, Libraries Linking Idaho: http://lili.org/

Illinois State Library, Research Databases (for state employees only;
other Illinois residents have access through their local university, college, K–12, or public libraries): http://www.cyberdriveillinois.com/
departments/library/databases/home.html

Indiana State Library, INSPIRE: http://www.in.gov/library/databases.html

State Library of Iowa, Online Resources: http://www.statelibraryofiowa
.org/services/online-resources/resources/index

Kansas State Library, Online Databases: http://kslib.info/221/Online
-Databases

Kentucky Department for Libraries and Archives, Research Databases
for State Employees: http://kdla.ky.gov/employees/databases/Pages/
default.aspx

Louisiana Library Connection: http://lalibcon.state.lib.la.us/

Maine InfoNet, MARVEL!: http://libraries.maine.edu/mainedatabases/

Maryland, Sailor Research Databases, http://www.sailor.lib.md.us/ser-
vices/databases/Default.aspx?id=56082

State Library of Massachusetts, Electronic Journals (and Databases):
http://rm8bp9xw4t.search.serialssolutions.com/?L=RM8BP9XW4T

Michigan eLibrary, Databases: http://mel.org/Databases

Electronic Library for Minnesota, Databases A–Z: http://www.elm4you
.org/

Mississippi Library Commission, MAGNOLIA: http://magnolia.msstate
.edu/

Missouri State Library, Find Articles (for state employees only; other Missouri residents have access through their local university, college, K–12,
or public libraries): http://mostate.libguides.com/reference/articles

Montana State Library, My Montana Library: http://mymontanalibrary
.org/

Nebraska Library Commission, NebraskAccess: http://nebraskaccess.ne
.gov/resources.asp

Nevada State Library and Archives, Research Databases: http://nsla.nv
.gov/Library/Library_Services/Research_Databases/

New Hampshire State Library, The Granite State's Information Connection: http://www.nh.gov/nhsl/nhewlink/public/

New Jersey State Library, JerseyClicks: http://www.jerseyclicks.org/homep-
ages/jclicks/jclicksclassic.asp

New Mexico State Library, El Portal: http://www.elportalnm.org/public
.php

New York State Library, Electronic Resources: http://www.nysl.nysed.gov/ elecres.htm

North Carolina, NC Live, Browse Resources A-Z, http://www.nclive.org/ browse

North Dakota State Library, Online Library Resources: http://www .library.nd.gov/onlineresources.html

Ohio Web Library: http://www.ohioweblibrary.org/sources/

Oklahoma Department of Libraries, Digital Prairie: http://www.odl.state .ok.us/prairie/index.htm

Oregon State Library, Libraries of Oregon: http://librariesoforegon.org/

Pennsylvania Department of Education, Office of Commonwealth Libraries, Power Library E-Resources: http://www.powerlibrary.org/

Rhode Island, Ocean State Libraries, Online Resources: http://oslri.org/ home/resources/

South Carolina State Library, Online Resources: http://statelibrary.sc.lib-guides.com/online-resources

South Dakota State Library, Online Resources: http://library.sd.gov/LIB/ ERD/onlineresources.aspx

Tennessee State Library and Archives, Tennessee Electronic Library (TEL): http://tntel.tnsos.org/

Texas State Library and Archives Commission, TexShare Databases: https://www.tsl.texas.gov/landing/tx-databases.html

Utah State Library, Pioneer: http://pioneer.utah.gov/research/databases/ index.html

Vermont Department of Libraries, Vermont Online Library: http://www .vtonlinelib.org/index.php

Library of Virginia, Using the Collections: http://www.lva.virginia.gov/ public/using_collections.asp

Washington: State residents have access through their local university, college, K–12, or public libraries.

West Virginia Library Commission, InfoDepot: http://wvinfodepot.org/

Wisconsin Department of Public Instruction, BadgerLink: http://www .badgerlink.dpi.wi.gov/

Wyoming State Library, GoWYLD, Wyoming's Portal to Knowledge and Learning: http://gowyld.net/

APPENDIX II

Encyclopedias and Other Reference Tools Freely Accessible on the Web

A.D.A.M. Medical Encyclopedia, from MedlinePlus: http://www.nlm.nih
.gov/medlineplus/encyclopedia.html
Ancient History Encyclopedia: http://www.ancient.eu/
BlackPast.org: http://www.blackpast.org/
Canadian Encyclopedia: http://www.thecanadianencyclopedia.com/en/
Digital Encyclopedia of George Washington: http://www.mountvernon.org/
research-collections/digital-encyclopedia/
Encyclopedia.com: http://www.encyclopedia.com/
Encyclopedia of Alabama: http://www.encyclopediaofalabama.org/
Encyclopedia of Arkansas History and Culture: http://www.encyclopediaof
arkansas.net/
Encyclopedia of Chicago: http://www.encyclopedia.chicagohistory.org/
Encyclopedia of Cleveland History: http://ech.case.edu/index.html
Encyclopedia of Detroit: http://detroithistorical.org/learn/encyclopedia
-of-detroit
Encyclopedia of Earth: http://www.eoearth.org/
Encyclopedia of Greater Philadelphia: http://philadelphiaencyclopedia.org/
Encyclopedia of Life: http://eol.org/
Encyclopedia of Mathematics: http://www.encyclopediaofmath.org/index
.php/Main_Page
Encyclopedia of Oklahoma History and Culture: http://www.okhistory.org/
publications/encyclopediaonline
Encyclopedia of the Great Plains: http://plainshumanities.unl.edu/
encyclopedia/
Encyclopedia of Virginia: http://www.encyclopediavirginia.org/
Encyclopedia Smithsonian: http://www.si.edu/encyclopedia
E-WV: The West Virginia Encyclopedia: http://www.wvencyclopedia.org/
Health Encyclopedia: http://www.pennmedicine.org/encyclopedia/

Health Encyclopedia: https://healthy.kaiserpermanente.org/health/care/ consumer/health-wellness/conditions-diseases/health-encyclopedia

HistoryLink: The Free Online Encyclopedia of Washington State History: http://www.historylink.org/index.cfm

Holocaust Encyclopedia: http://www.ushmm.org/learn/holocaust -encyclopedia

Jewish Women: A Comprehensive Historical Encyclopedia: http://jwa.org/ encyclopedia

KnowLA: Encyclopedia of Louisiana: http://knowla.org/

National Science Digital Library: https://nsdl.oercommons.org/

NCPedia (North Carolina): http://ncpedia.org/

New Georgia Encyclopedia: http://www.georgiaencyclopedia.org/

ONE: Online Nevada Encyclopedia: http://www.onlinenevada.org/

Oregon Encyclopedia: http://oregonencyclopedia.org/

Stanford Encyclopedia of Philosophy: http://plato.stanford.edu/

Tennessee Encyclopedia of History and Culture: http://tennesseeencyclopedia .net/

Utah eMedia: https://eq.uen.org/emedia/home.do

Wikipedia: http://en.wikipedia.org/wiki/Main_Page

WyoHistory.org, Encyclopedia: http://www.wyohistory.org/encyclopedia

APPENDIX III

Freely Available Information Resources by Subject

FACTS, DEFINITIONS, EVENTS, QUOTATIONS

Dictionary.com: http://dictionary.reference.com/
Bartleby—Great Books Online: http://www.bartleby.com/
Infoplease: http://www.infoplease.com/
Thesaurus.com: http://www.thesaurus.com/

GOVERNMENT, LAW, POLITICS

Congress.gov: https://www.congress.gov/
Cornell Law School Legal Information Institute: http://www.law.cornell .edu/
Oyez Project: http://www.oyez.org/
United States Government Manual: http://www.usgovernmentmanual .gov/
World Factbook: https://www.cia.gov/library/publications/resources/the -world-factbook/

HISTORY

Columbia University Libraries Digital Collections: http://library.columbia .edu/find/digital-collections.html
Harvard University Library Open Collections Program: http://ocp.hul .harvard.edu/
Library of Congress Digital Collections: http://www.loc.gov/collections
LLILAS Benson Digital Collections: http://lanic.utexas.edu/project/lbdc/

Media History Digital Library: http://mediahistoryproject.org/
New York Public Library's Digital Schomburg: http://www.nypl.org/
    locations/tid/64/node/65914

SCIENCE, GEOGRAPHY, MEDICINE

Arizona Sonora Desert Museum Digital Library: http://desertmuseum
    digitallibrary.org/public/index.php
MedlinePlus: http://www.nlm.nih.gov/medlineplus/
National Atlas: http://nationalatlas.gov/index.html
National Science Digital Library: http://nsdl.org/
Public Library of Science: http://www.plos.org/
SciTech Connect: http://www.osti.gov/scitech/

ART, LITERATURE, MUSIC

HathiTrust: http://www.hathitrust.org/
Internet Archive: https://archive.org/
National Gallery of Art: https://images.nga.gov/en/page/show_home_page
    .html
National Jukebox: http://www.loc.gov/jukebox/about
Project Gutenberg: http://www.gutenberg.org/wiki/Main_Page

Index

About the Author

As a member of the faculty of the University of Arizona School of Information, **Cheryl Knott** teaches courses in online searching, government information, and other topics related to information access. She earned her PhD in library and information science at the University of Texas while working as a reference librarian at the Perry-Castañeda Library.